TIME TEAM 96

The Site Reports

Written by Tim Taylor, series producer

Archaeological consultant: Mick Aston

CHANNEL FOUR TELEVISION

CONTENTS

THE TIME TEAM

Tony Robinson, the series presenter, is probably best known as Baldrick in *Blackadder* and as the Sheriff of Nottingham in *Maid Marian and Her Merry Men*, which he also writes. He has a keen interest in history and archaeology – he is president of the Young Archaeologists' Club – and is particularly fascinated by ancient Greece and the biblical lands of the Middle East.

Mick Aston, the team leader, has been involved with archaeology for more than 30 years, and is currently Reader in Archaeology at the University of Bristol. He has written numerous books and articles, including *Interpreting the Landscape*, the standard work on landscape archaeology. To date, he has appeared on four series on archaeology for Channel 4.

Victor Ambrus, a Fellow of the Royal Academy of Arts, is a freelance illustrator with more than 250 books to his credit, most on historical subjects. He has twice won the Kate Greenaway Award for best illustrated children's book of the year.

Robin Bush, formerly Deputy County Archivist for Somerset, is a freelance lecturer, historian and broadcaster. An expert in genealogy and on the history of early emigration to the United States, he is author of numerous books on local history, including a definitive guide to Somerset.

Phil Harding is a field archaeologist with the Trust for Wessex Archaeology. He has worked in archaeology for over 25 years, and is a recognised expert in flint knapping and the Palaeolithic period.

Carenza Lewis has been a field archaeologist for the Royal Commission on Historic Monuments for England (RCHME) for over ten years. A specialist in the medieval period and in historic landscapes, she has worked extensively in Wessex and co-edited a collection of essays on the medieval landscape of this part of England.

The *TIME TEAM (left to right)*: Mick Aston, Victor Ambrus, Robin Bush, Phil Harding, Tony Robinson and Carenza Lewis.

BOLEIGH

CORNWALL

WHAT MIGHT HAVE HAPPENED

They lay in the dark cave and waited for the light of the rising sun to pierce the passage. These were dangerous times, and it felt natural to come to the place that their ancestors had revered – where shelter and safety combined with a feeling of being close to those spirits of earth and water that promised continuity. Their ancestors had chosen well. The site of the small settlement was near water, which had also broken down the tin ore needed to make their tools. Some of their number knew the secrets of taking the small specks of black tin, combining it with the green-veined copper that ran in the local stone, and making bronze. The tin could also be traded for the metal of the latest technology: iron. Farming on such thin soil had to be subsidised, and the trade in tin was the answer. From the earliest times, boats from the warmer lands to the south had arrived and exchanged wine, oil and beads for the humble tin that lay, black and heavy, in the stream beds.

The inhabitants had expanded their settlement and brought in new animals. The families had grown, and the community had decided to extend the dark passages in the earth. They invited back the specialist builders, and new shafts were constructed for ventilation and the chamber widened.

Within the settlement, they felt safe – the fires burned and the grain was ground. New pots were made and offerings left in the darkness of their underground sanctuary at the heart of their village.

(Left) The fogou entrance, seen from the inside. *(Mick Aston)*
(Above) Victor's reconstruction of the Iron Age settlement, the inhabitants of which would have created and used the fogou. *(Mick Aston)*

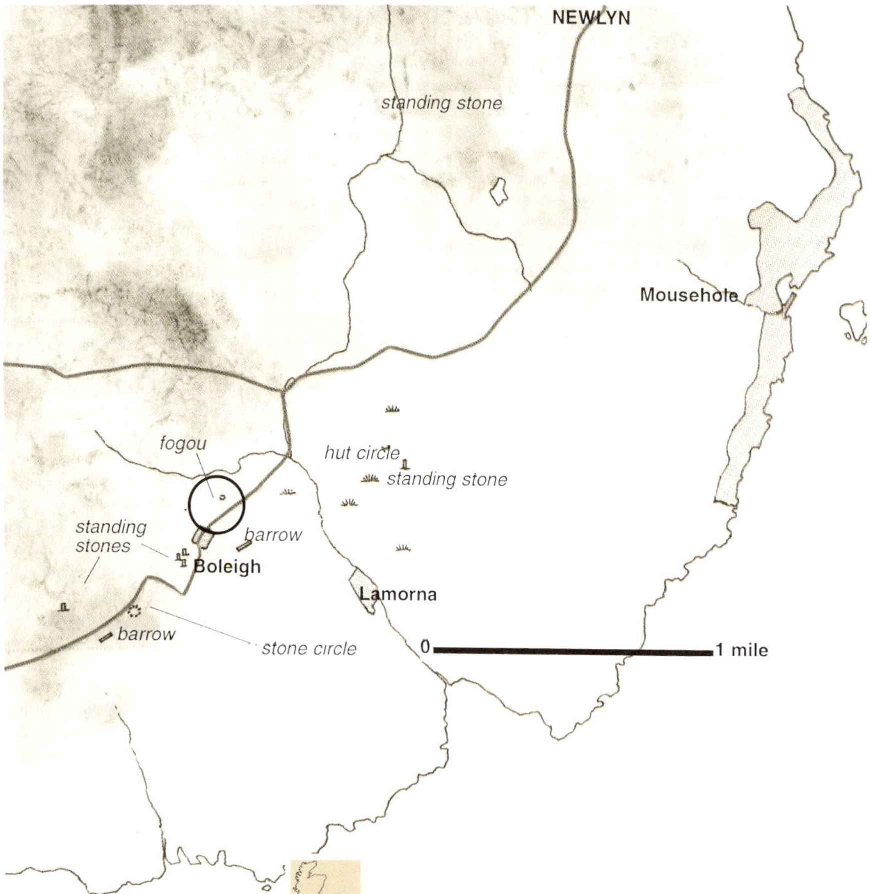

WHY WE WENT THERE

The far west of Cornwall – West Penwith – has a unique and rich archaeological history. Standing stones, stone circles, prehistoric settlements and traces of the Bronze Age and Iron Age are more common here than in any other part of England. As you travel along the modern A30, you can still imagine a time when the Hayle and Marazion lowlands would have been wetter and how this would have divided West Penwith from the main south-west land mass.

The lovely Lamorna Cove is only a short distance from the Boleigh fogou, which is at the far end of the valley (top/centre of the photograph). *(Mick Aston)*

The earliest historical reference to the British Isles notes the importance of trade in tin with the inhabitants of this area. The reference occurs in the writings of the Greek-Sicilian historian Diodorus Siculus who, in about 100 BC, quoted an even earlier traveller around the coasts of Europe – the Greek navigator known as Pytheas of Marseilles. He is believed to have visited many parts of northern Europe in c. 400 BC, and referred to the inhabitants of the 'British promontory Belerium' who, due to their contact with merchants over a long period, were 'more civilised and courteous to strangers than the rest are'. He described their skill in extracting tin and how this was turned into ingots and transported to an island called 'Ictis', which modern historians regard as being St Michael's Mount.

Our decision to go to Cornwall meant not only that we would undoubtedly find a wealth of ancient sites, but also that we would be entering an area where archaeology has encountered New Age spirituality. Many of the archaeological sites there have been adopted by the followers of New Age and 'earth mystery' cults. In some cases, this has meant that the sites have been better cared for than before, their purpose redefined for a new generation. However, the relationship between archaeologists and the New Agers has not always been a comfortable one.

Archaeologists need to look at sites with a hard-headed pragmatism that can sometimes collide with a New Age desire to invest these places with a power and a meaning that may have little basis in archaeological fact. It is often assumed that archaeologists are all too ready to debunk mystery and legend-based interpretations, and this has meant that the two sides often fail to appreciate each other's insights. In the more extreme cases, sites have actually been damaged by people with an over-zealous desire to 'recreate' spiritual events that have little connection with the monuments' real past.

However, occasionally there has been a sympathetic interaction between the two sides, and the site to which we had been invited was a case in point. Approximately two miles from Penzance, near the beautiful Lamorna Cove, is a small settlement called Boleigh (pronounced 'bo-lay'). Here Joe May has founded the Centre for Alternative Education and Research (CAER). Behind his home is a well-preserved example of one of the most mysterious monuments of Cornwall's prehistory – a fogou (pronounced 'fog-oo'). Fogous, from the Cornish for 'cave', are deep underground caves or passages that are, in England and Wales, unique to this area. They are associated with late Bronze Age/early Iron Age sites in Ireland (where they are numerous), Brittany and here in Cornwall.

There are at least 11 fogous left in West Penwith, and more than that have been 'lost'. According to conventional archaeology, these fascinating structures were intended for refuge or storage purposes. For instance, they often have narrow sections – 'creeps' – that appear to be defensive in nature, allowing one person to keep at bay an attacking force. The alternative view is that they had a spiritual purpose, enabling people to get closer to the spirits of the earth,

and were constructed so that village priests, or shamans, could contact their sources of power. Joe May had been visited by members of the Native American tradition, who pointed out the similarities between the Cornish fogous and their own structures known as *kivas*, which also had a spiritual purpose.

As usual with many monuments of the prehistoric period, so little is actually known that interpretation is difficult. (Maybe TIME TEAM's work will help!). Ian Cooke, a local author and authority on fogous, proposes in his book, *Mother and Son – The Cornish Fogou*, that the majority of these structures are aligned to major settings and risings of the midwinter/summer sun. Ian had agreed to join us during the excavations, and we were also delighted that two dowsers, Hamish Miller and Barbara Russell, were to try out their skills in the somewhat hectic atmosphere of a TIME TEAM weekend

Day One

We began our work with two main aims: first, to see if the fogou had some hidden, longer sections, possibly heading under Joe May's garden (he had alerted us to this possibility); and second, to see if we could find any evidence of the settlement where the people who built the fogou had lived. In addition, we had been asked by Joe to see if we could find any trace of a figure said to have been carved on the stone at the entrance to the fogou. Earlier antiquarians – those amateur students of antiquities who were the precursors of today's trained archaeologists – had drawn what appears to be a Celtic figure holding a snake and a spear. Outside our main area of investigation, we had been asked to see if our geophysics team, led by John Gater of Geophysics Surveys of Bradford, could locate another fogou at a farm site at Treveneague, north-east of Penzance, which had once been excavated by the antiquarian J. T. Blight but the exact location of which had been forgotten.

We had two sources of information to guide us. Recent excavations at Halligye (east of Boleigh) by Bill Startin had shown that fogous tend to be an integral part of a settlement. We hoped that the small walls and ditches that appeared to surround the Boleigh fogou would be the remains of the wall that once enclosed a settlement. Stuart Ainsworth – who, with Bernard Thomason, was representing the Royal Commission on Historic Monuments for England (RCHME) on this TIME TEAM series – was keen to survey these features and to match them up with an earlier survey that Robin had been studying.

Our second source was the work of the antiquarian J. T. Blight (1835–1911). Cornwall's antiquarians had, as elsewhere, their fair share of eccentric visionaries, whose quest to locate all manner of historical and less-than-historical figures – from Jesus to King Arthur – in the landscape make them a good source for those with a more imaginative response to the past. However, some antiquarians, at great personal cost, mapped out the basic prehistoric structures in Britain, many of which have since disappeared, and for this reason alone, we owe them a great debt of gratitude.

J. T. Blight was one of a number of Cornish antiquarians to realise the richness of the prehistoric remains on their doorstep. He made meticulous drawings and maps, but the lack of interest or belief in his theories and the absence of a rich sponsor for his work gradually got the better of him and he ended his life in a house for the insane in Bodmin. He had, however, visited Boleigh in 1876 and left drawings of the fogou that seemed to indicate a surrounding structure. Would his drawings match up with Stuart's survey? Tantalisingly, Joe May had also found another old reference to the Boleigh fogou, which said that it was of such a length that an arrow fired into the darkness would fail to reach the end.

Any excavations we might make would be limited by the fact that an area around the fogou and the structure itself are scheduled ancient monuments. This meant that, although the surrounding area had been defined fairly close to the fogou, we could not start from the fogou and excavate outwards. If we did, we would run the risk of damaging a unique monument.

(Top left) Dowser Hamish Miller begins work. *(Mick Aston)*
(Above centre) Excavators work in the trench across the probable Iron Age boundary, unearthing the remains of prehistoric houses. *(Mick Aston)*

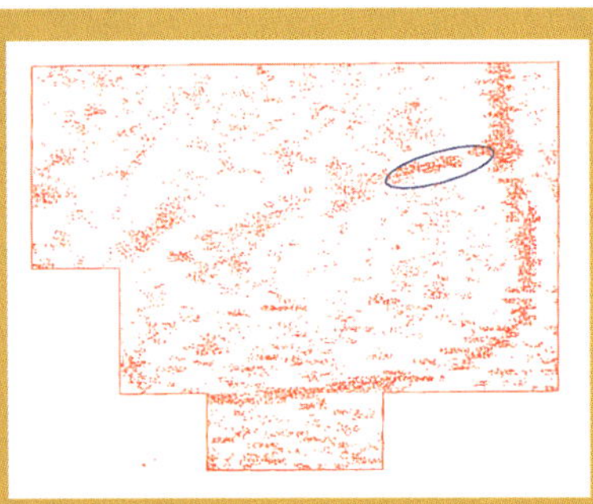

Geophysics

'Geophysics' are the physics of the earth, and today archaeologists and others have a group of geophysical techniques that can help them find structures of interest below the surface of the ground. The most common of these are magnetometry and resistivity.

In the former, the earth's magnetic field is measured together with any effects that structures in the ground may have on it. Walls, pits and ditches can all affect the readings, and these can then be plotted, producing a sort of underground, or subsurface, map. With resistivity, the electrical resistance of the soil and any buried features in it is measured: where there are buried pits and ditches, there is little resistance, whereas walls and stone give great resistance.

(Above) Magnetic results showing location of fogou (ringed) within an enclosing ditch. The break in the anomaly marks the entrance. *(Geophysical Surveys of Bradford)*

Our geophysics investigation (*see box above*) began on Joe's lawn. Earlier in the day, Joe and Tony had done a bit of initial survey work by jumping up and down, then listening for noises that might indicate cavities. The more scientific approach produced an immediate result. Much to everyone's delight, we were looking at a strong anomaly (an odd or unexpected feature) that appeared to head towards the fogou, curving under Joe's lawn towards the outer edge of the garden terrace. Naturally we all became excited, and after consulting with Nick Johnson – County Archaeologist and head of the Cornwall Archaeological Unit, who were on hand to give their expert local advice – we decided to place a trench where the anomaly appeared to turn.

Carenza and Stuart had already decided that a trench across the boundary edge on the opposite side of the fogou might help us to locate the exterior wall of the settlement. Most Cornish settlements from this prehistoric period had strong granite foundations, on top of which were constructed heavy walls built from the natural boulders that cover the landscape. The Boleigh fogou certainly has the appearance of having been built by experts in the craft of drystone walling. They used a technique called 'cut and cover': after digging a trench, a passage was formed by building two walls of coarse stones that sloped inwards towards the top, which was capped by huge slabs of granite weighing many tons. It is hard to believe that such a structure would have been built simply to store supplies.

The garden trench proceeded quickly, partly due to an absence of finds. This was alarming, for if we were inside a settlement area, we should at least be turning up pottery sherds (broken pieces of pottery) and the odd bone, but all we had by the end of the day were heaps of Joe's garden soil.

Trench two appeared far more promising. With help from the Cornwall Archaeological Unit excavators, we shifted a fair amount of top soil and came to large blocks of stone, clearly placed in the ground by humans. The stones appeared to be set in a line along a ridge that skirted the edge of the hill, with other stones heading towards the fogou itself.

By the end of the day, we had discovered the source of John's anomaly in trench one. At the bottom of the deep excavation, which had chopped a not-inconsiderable hole in Joe's lawn, sat an iron water pipe. Unknown to Joe, a previous owner of the property must have decided to install irrigation for the gardens below the main house. Not only did the pipe align with the fogou, but it had a wonderful curve that seemed to mimic the shape of extensions found at other fogous. The

iron pipe itself, possibly still containing some water, gave a strong geophysics response that was out of all proportion to its size. A classic piece of archaeological deception! Day Two would have to start with a rethink.

Day Two

The day began with a redoubled effort to locate evidence of the settlement in trench two. Phil had to be called away from this work, for we had been joined by two local experts in the skills of tin panning and smelting. During the period 400–250 BC, this area of Cornwall had increased its contacts with traders from the Continent, and the readily available supply of tin – an ore not commonly found – created new wealth for many Cornish settlements. Tin was the essential ingredient that, mixed with copper, produced bronze, a material that was still in use throughout the Iron Age. It was fascinating to see how the small

(Top right) Victor Ambrus at the fogou's 'creep' – the narrow section that was easily defensible. *(Mick Aston)*
(Above right) One of the sherds of Iron Age pottery found at the site. *(Mick Aston)*

pebbles of tin could be sorted from the river gravels. This and the smelting would have been carried out in most Cornish settlements of this time.

However, our main concern early on Day Two was that we appeared to be outside the settlement area. It was at this stage that Stuart's work on Blight's drawings, as well as his own survey and observation, bore fruit. By matching up all available information on the computer and reducing it to the same scale, Stuart made an exciting discovery. Blight's measurements appeared to line up accurately with a set of ridges and walls that were much closer to the fogou than we had expected. We had taken the edge of the settlement to be Joe's garden wall, beyond which was a steep drop, and, perhaps influenced by the hollow noises created by Tony and Joe's jumping, had accepted that the garden was inside the settlement boundary.

Stuart's work led Mick and Carenza to narrow their focus, realising that the settlement area was actually much closer to the fogou. It was soon apparent that one of the reasons for the lack of finds was the fact that, when Joe's home had been built, a large proportion of the hilltop had been shaved off to create the foundations. Had this removed all signs of settlement around the fogou? Trench two now gave us the answers. The surface stones that we had found there continued down to become part of more substantial structures. As we extended the excavation towards the edge of the scheduled area, we began to uncover a settlement layer that contained much darker soil and – at last – large amounts of Iron Age pottery.

Our hunt for the possible lost tunnels of the fogou also led us to take up the offer of local dowsers Hamish Miller and Barbara Russell who, braving the noise of the excavations, attempted to locate areas that might contain fogou extensions. Hamish's work, begun before Stuart's revelations, had concentrated on the garden, where he felt some energy that might indicate that the fogou did continue further. A small trial excavation failed to locate any feature, although on the final day near to the fogou itself, Stuart would locate a set of stones that seemed to head off in the direction that Hamish had indicated.

Stuart Ainsworth surveying inside the Boleigh fogou. *(Mick Aston)*

A third trench was now begun opposite trench two, across the line of the small oval shape that, based on Stuart's work with the maps, he, Carenza and Mick now felt was the boundary. This involved digging up part of Joe's garden path, but his keenness to find out as much as possible about the fogou overcame any worries about the temporary disruption of his garden. This trench began to produce finds almost immediately, including a broken stone, that would have been used to rub grain on a saddle-shaped stone called a quern. This object and some other pieces of Iron Age pottery began to establish a good date for trench three.

Two things were now becoming apparent: the quantity of Iron Age pottery and other finds clearly showed that we had located areas of habitation contemporary with the fogou, but this settlement was much smaller than we had expected – typically such settlements are larger.

Day Three

On this, the final day, Nick Johnson and his team began the critical business of recording the evidence in the trenches. John Gater and the geophysics team also visited Treveneague and had returned with a clear printout of the 'lost' fogou – the first time that this structure had been accurately located and seen since Blight's excavations in the 19th century.

Once all of TIME TEAM's work at Boleigh has been assessed, it may add a little more to our knowledge of these unique monuments. The fogous still, however, retain their mystery. Although we were unable to find any clear evidence of Joe's Celtic figure, we all felt – particularly when we crouched inside the fogou, staring out at the shafts of sunlight emphasising the edges of the massive entrance stones – that there was a lot more to these structures than could be explained by conventional archaeology.

Final thoughts from Mick

I had been to this fogou at Boleigh many years ago, when I was a young student looking at the archaeology of West Penwith and trying to see as many types of sites as possible. So it was good to visit it again, but even better to be able to show how it fitted into a contemporary settlement site. Most exciting, however, was to findthe 'lost' fogou at Treveneague – a major new discovery for archaeology and one of so few sites of this type in England.

STANTON HARCOURT

OXFORDSHIRE

WHAT MIGHT HAVE HAPPENED

For the hunters, the trail across the endless sequence of small islands covering the waterlogged valley had proved a frustrating one. The big floods had not come that year, but the ground was still treacherous, and the mammoth, wounded and lame, had dragged itself from thicket to boggy swamp with its last reserves of energy. Although less formidable than the larger elephants, it could still lash out with its tusks, but the group, experienced in driving prey like this, were patient – the land wasn't cold and there was plenty of small game and fish to supply their needs. As one of their number prepared the large flint handaxes, the sharp edges glinting in the last light of the sunset, they knew it was just a matter of time.

Across the distant plain, a herd of wild horses broke cover and ran down into the valley. Bison grazed by the river, safe on the harder ground by the channel's edge. The mammoth's injury had been the chance that the hunters had been waiting for. At daybreak, the sharpened sticks and flint tools would do their job, and once they closed in for the kill, they knew that their families would not go hungry that winter. Now, as night descended, they heard the dying groans of the mammoth as it settled down into the holding mud.

Victor's reconstruction of the Stanton Harcourt landscape 200,000 years ago, with a mammoth in the foreground and the river running from left to right

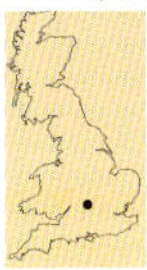

WHY WE WENT THERE

The excavation of gravel at this site in southern England created a rich by-product for archaeologists. The gravel had overlain the muds and silts of the Paleolithic period (Old Stone Age), which contained plants, animals and stone tools from about 200,000 years ago.

For several years, archaeologist Kate Scott and geologist Christine Buckingham, co-directors of the site, had been working at the gravel pit at Stanton Harcourt, a few miles west of Oxford, with fairly limited resources, although this site may prove to be one of the richest in the remains of mammoth bones. Assuming the bone spread is consistent across the site, there could be as many as 5000 mammoths buried under the gravel. Yet, soon, the land is to become a landfill – hence the invitation to TIME TEAM.

Another fascination of this site is that it might provide evidence of a new interglacial period. During the Ice Age, sheets of ice advanced from the north and retreated. During some of the retreats (or interglacials), which lasted tens of thousands of years, there was enough time for a top soil and vegetation to form in the warmer climate, and this enabled some plant and animal species to extend their range northwards. Here at Stanton Harcourt, evidence had been found of species such as elephants mixed with mammoths. The latter are usually believed to have lived in colder climates, but here they were experiencing a warmer period. There are signs that they may have adapted to this warmth by developing finer teeth for chewing the lusher foliage.

Kate and Christine place the Stanton Harcourt interglacial at around 200,000 BC – in the middle of the Wolstonian glacial, which lasted from the end of the Hoxian interglacial in around 330,000 BC, to the beginning of the Ipswichian interglacial, around 135,000 BC. These strange names, nominated by geologists, reflect the locations where the geological deposits that helped to date the event were first discovered. For instance, 'Wolstonian', the name for the penultimate glacial period in northern Europe, is named after the 'type-site' of Wolston in Warwickshire. The situation is further complicated by the fact that different continents have given the glaciations different names. In Europe, the 'Wolstonian' is called the 'Saalian' and, in North America, the 'Illinonian'. It's perfectly possible that, if Kate and Christina are right, their interglacial could be called the 'Stantonian'!

The essential problem faced by archaeologists and geologists alike is that these events occurred so long ago that evidence is limited, especially since glaciers act like bulldozers and can remove previous landscapes completely. It was once thought that, after humans came to Britain, there were three ice ages and three warm periods (interglacials). However, some people now believe that there may have been as many as eight interglacials. This controversy provides a rich breeding ground for academic strife, with various groups claiming to have discovered new glacial events and others disagreeing.

Kate's main evidence for Stanton Harcourt's interglacial – the animal and plant remains – face two challenges that are common to the study of the Palaeolithic. The first is demonstrating that the evidence was more or less *in situ* and had not originated miles away or been deposited there by a previous period's meltwater. During the Ice Age, a vast amount of ice and water was washing around, and this could carry objects for hundreds of miles. In addition, material from an earlier period might have been washed on to a site as a glacier melted. So it is necessary to examine each element of evidence to see how far it may have travelled from its point of origin.

The second challenge is to provide enough good environmental data to

One of the Stone Age handaxes found at Stanton Harcourt. *(Mick Aston)*

convince oneself and others that the necessary change in climate and the influx of appropriate species both took place. This usually requires a detailed assessment of pollen, seeds, insects and the like. On a site where every shovelful of mud appears to reveal the fascinating remains of a mammoth, it had clearly been difficult for Kate to devote time to collecting environmental data in sufficient amounts to prove her case.

The mammoth bones were not the only distraction on the site. There was also the tantalising prospect that we might find human remains. Already nine Stone Age tools had been discovered, including some handaxes. The condition of a few of these suggested that they may not have travelled far. Could there also be some actual traces of our most ancient ancestors? The earliest remains of human beings in Britain were found in Boxgrove in West Sussex and have been dated to 500,000 BC, and the next oldest were those found in Swanscombe in Kent, from 300,000 BC. It is believed that the appearance of the Swanscombe individuals would have been similar to Neanderthal man, but Kate suggested that the occupants of Stanton Harcourt at a later period may have been a more gracile form of *Homo sapiens*. However, as yet no evidence of human bones had come to light. Examples from this period are so rare that such a discovery would be of immense importance.

Kate and Christine also needed to get a clear idea of the structure of the site they were working on. The landscape at Stanton Harcourt 200,000 years ago would have been dominated by a deep, wide river with a channel of a minimum width of 60 m (200 ft), running from east to west. After the water receded, a smaller river occupied this channel, which split at various points to create small islands, and other areas became marsh or swamp. The edge of the river is where we were most likely to find good environmental evidence, so it was critical to map the site and use geophysics to locate these old river beds. This would be the first time that our geophysics team had been asked to locate 'palaeo-channels', as they are called. The hope was that there would be a difference between the polarisation of the river clays and that of the gravels, which could be detected by magnetometry or resistivity.

Day One

While the geophysics team went to work, Carenza began examining our aerial photographs, and Stuart started a GPS survey in order to create a 3D model of the site. Phil and Mick joined Kate to excavate a channel edge in the hope that some good environmental evidence might appear. We had invited Professor Russell Coope and Dr Mike Allan to join us. Russell is an expert on beetles and other insects, and Mike would be working on the seeds and plants. Later on in the weekend, they would be joined by an expert in identifying woodland species.

Our first excavation quickly uncovered the root of a mammoth tusk, which was accompanied by the skull of a bison and other bones. All bones had to be examined closely to assess the species – a single bone could mean the addition of another animal on Kate's list, which already included mammoth, elephant, lion, hyena, horse, bison and bear. Bones can also show marks that may indicate the cause of death or the fact that the animal had been butchered – a sign of human presence. However, a bone tumbling in a flooded river can acquire all sorts of gouges and scratches that are difficult to distinguish from deliberate cuts. In addition, butchery does not necessarily leave marks on bone.

The tusk we were uncovering was in remarkably good condition, which pointed to it having come from an animal that died relatively close to the site. Just how so many bones came to be deposited here is open to interpretation. One theory is that the Stanton Harcourt remains were deposited by a catastrophic flood. This is based on a number of clues: the relatively undamaged nature of the bones; the fact that tusks are buried whole and are mixed in with large tree debris, which would have had to occur quickly; the fact that the geological deposits are relatively coarse; and the scattered presence of molluscs and Jurassic bivalves that have come from deposits some miles east of Stanton Harcourt. All this seems to indicate that an incredible amount of water flooded into the channel over a short period, possibly as little as a day.

Back at the excavation, Russell was taking samples of environmental evidence from the trench, where he

GPS

'Global positioning by satellite', a system that uses US military technology by tracking up to nine satellites in space to locate positions on the ground. It is astonishingly accurate, enabling a point anywhere on the earth's surface to be located within 5 mm in plan and 10 mm in the vertical plane. The other main advantage is its speed – the computations are carried out at walking pace, enabling a large amount of land to be surveyed within a short time. The coordinates obtained, fed into a computer, generate a three-dimensional map.

Kate Scott excavating the mammoth tusk and bison skull. *(Mick Aston)*

had found a rich band of darker material that he hoped would contain plant and animal remains. He then extracted these – a sort of panning for archaeological gold. The first part of the process involved removing the fine silts and sands with copious amounts of water poured through 300-micron mesh sieves. The soupy mixture that remained was mixed with paraffin, which causes any seeds and beetle remains to float to the surface. Russell then decanted these and bathed them in washing-up liquid to remove any remaining paraffin. The remains, floated in alcohol, were separated out with tweezers. Russell would give us his results the next day.

In the trench, Phil was revealing more and more of our mammoth tusk, which gave us an idea of how large these animals were. Mammoths were part of the elephant family. In the early stages of their evolutionary life, they were huge, but gradually they became the size of modern Indian elephants. The Stanton mammoths – which, Kate believes, may have been an isolated population cut off by a rise in sea levels – were even smaller with small chewing teeth, but they still had large tusks. They shared this environment with straight-tusked elephants twice their size. It is fairly easy to distinguish between mammoth and elephant teeth, and with luck, we would uncover some examples as our excavation progressed.

At the end of the first day, we were joined by the volunteers from the Earth Watch charity, who would be helping Kate and the team throughout the weekend. In our incident tent, the geophysical data and survey material were beginning to be plotted on the computers, and the environmental finds were being processed.

Day Two

Despite a change in the immediate climate – which Tony described as the onset of another glacial period – we were keen to look at both the survey and environmental results.

Having collected a large number of beetle remains from his samples, Russell praised the virtue of this humble insect as a diagnostic tool for archaeologists. Beetle remains are amazingly indestructible – even after 200,000 years, we were able to distinguish pieces of shell and body parts – and they are also specific to certain environments and climates. Some beetles keep to woods and shrubs, some are keener on river margins and animal dung, some with more dubious taste like rotting bodies, and still others prefer warmer climates to colder ones. This means that finding a good range of beetles can help to build up a detailed picture of a particular environment. For instance, Russell had discovered a beetle called *Bembidion varium* of the Carabidae family, which indicated a warmer climate; a member of the Histeridae family called *Hister quadrinaculatus*, which signalled the presence of dead bodies with flies; and *Aphodius fasciatus*, of the Scarabaeidae family, which liked the dung of large herbivores – probably our mammoths. And (if you've finished your dinner) he also had a happy little creature called *Dermestes murinus* that is specific to dead corpses already eaten by maggots!

John Gater was also in a good mood because he had some clear geophysics readings that would help to locate the new channels. When some of the scrub was removed from the centre of the site, he would be able to extend the survey. As if to emphasise the importance of the river margins, Kate took us to the north end of the site to show us a small area where part of one had already been exposed.

As the plastic sheets protecting it were peeled back, we saw part of a riverbank that had last seen the light of day in the Palaeolithic era. Branches, shrubs and roots could easily be seen, and Rowena Gale, our specialist in identifying wood remains, took samples to help identify the tree species. In addition, there was a small collection of shells called *Corbicula fluminalis*, which, because they occurred in only a few of the interglacials that have taken place in Britain, were important if Kate was to prove the existence of a new one. Russell informed us that, today, the shells are common in the Nile delta, implying that the creatures that were housed in them had a preference for a warmer climate. These delicate objects were not only intact and upright but also in a family group, with tiny young *Corbicula* attached to the fringes. This was clear evidence that we were looking at the original land surface – the *Corbicula* would not have survived like this if they had been deposited by flood water from elsewhere.

We had also asked Phil to show Tony how to make a handaxe, a tool that was used for butchery and was

Sieving a mud sample looking for the remains of prehistoric snails. *(Mick Aston)*

indispensable for dismembering large carcases. The axes found at Stanton Harcourt were not made from local stone. The nearest source was 30 miles away, and it is possible that they were knapped from flint nodules carried to our site – exactly the way Phil was going to work. The handaxes from Stanton were described by Kate as 'Acheulian', a name derived from the place in France where many such axes were found.

Differences in stone tools can help archaeologists approximately date the sites where such evidence is found. Each stage of development tends to be characterised by a more sophisticated technique, particularly with regard to using flint more economically. One way of analysing a random group of stone tools would to imagine the amount of work required to create each implement. For instance, it takes only a few strikes of stone against stone to make an Olduvai pebble tool, whereas to produce a flaked and ground Tievebulliagh axe would take a great deal more work. This factor, along with an analysis of shape and of associated finds, can be employed to place a stone tool in a chronology.

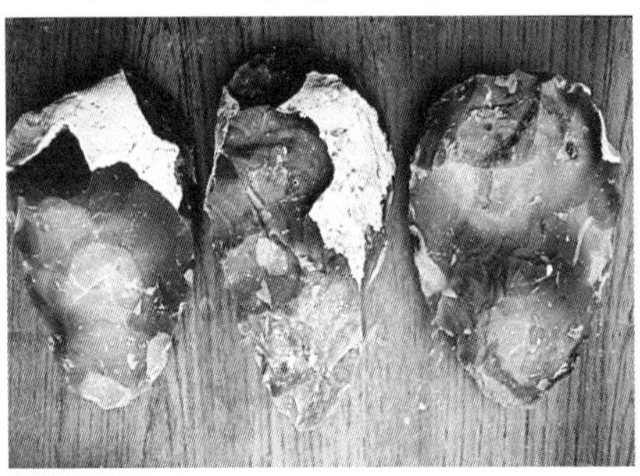

In describing a range of tools – illustrating the development of stone implements, for example – we are creating a *typology*. This is an important method for archaeologists as a clear and obvious typology for axes, arrowheads, pottery or any other artefact allows them to date (or at least place in archaeological sequence) objects from other sites. In some cases – as with handaxes – a typology may cover thousands of years, or it might involve small changes in the surface design of pottery that have occurred over the period of only a few years.

The earliest stone tools were created in Africa 2.4 million years ago. These were simple pebbles with the occasional flake knocked off them to create an

edge, and were used by the earliest form of humans, *Homo habilis*. A new form of human being, *Homo erectus*, spread out of Africa into the rest of the world (excluding the Americas), carrying with them a new kind of stone-tool technique, which we have called 'Acheulian', which produced the classic bi-facial handaxes, flaked on both sides. This period, lasting until c. 200,000 BC, is known as the Lower Palaeolithic. When people first came to Britain, they had already been making handaxes for about 800,000 years and so were getting quite good at it!

Homo sapiens emerged in about 200,000 BC, and conveniently we have a new kind of stone tool being produced called Levallois, after the region of France where the tools were first recognised. The creation of these involved preparing a core from which flakes were struck, and relied on the knapper being able to predict and control the shape of the final flake before it was struck off the core – a difficult thing to do. This technique was present in the Middle Palaeolithic, from 200,000 to 40,000 BC, so it is possible that the events at Stanton Harcourt occurred soon after the technique arrived in Britain.

Around 35,000 BC, Upper Palaeolithic tools began to be made using an advanced technology involving the creation of a series of blades from a core, which could then be used separately as individual knives or scrapers, or combined in a handle as a composite tool. According to Phil, this technology is characterised by the most economic use of the raw material: a single core converted into blades will produce the maximum length of cutting edge. It was also the first time that standardised tools were made.

(Top left) Phil Harding flint knapping – that is, making a handaxe. *(Mick Aston)*
(Above left) Three handaxes: the results of Phil's labours. *(Mick Aston)*
(Above) One of the huge mammoth teeth found at Stanton Harcourt. *(Mick Aston)*

In about 10,000 BC – in the Middle Stone Age, or Mesolithic – microliths appeared: small stone tools that required skilled retouching, and which form the basis for many composite tools including barbed spears and arrowheads or points. In the Neolithic (c. 4000–2400 BC), ground and polished stone axes were made – a nice example of which was the Tievebulliagh axe that the TIME TEAM would later find in Navan in Northern Ireland (*see* p. 31). Grinding strengthened the edges of these.

There is a reasonable chance that any stone axe or core or blade found on a site would fit somewhere into this recognisable time line. It takes an expert like Phil to be certain, but most people can understand the main differences once they have seen a few good examples.

Kate and Christine now had to make a critical decision. ARC, the company that owned the gravel pit, had agreed to provide a massive digger that could clear a strip across the site that would be wide enough to locate more areas of the original land surface. However, it was likely that, in the process, this would destroy some bone remains. Kate and Christine knew that they could go on excavating bones on this site for ever and still not answer their crucial questions. They would have to decide what to do by the next morning.

At the end of the day, the trench produced our first mammoth tooth. Mammoths had two massive teeth on each side of the jaw at a time, new ones erupting through at the back of the mouth and moving slowly forward as wearing of the old teeth took place. Our tooth was clearly smaller and less corrugated than an elephant's tooth.

Day Three

Kate and Christine had made their decision and the digger was moving in. In the end, they felt that the chance of finding new areas of environmental evidence and locating the river channels was worth the risk of losing the odd bone.The digger proceeded across the landscape, carefully watched by Phil and Kate.

New evidence came in from Mike Allan about the pollen and seed varieties that he had identified, adding to a list of plants for the site that already included meadow sweet, saxifrage, scabious, valerian and buttercup. He was also beginning to build up a good collection of snail remains, including the *Pupilla mascara* that likes dry grassland. Brian Irving, an expert on amphibians whom we had also brought in, had found evidence of pike and eels, as well as a pelvis bone from a tree frog (*Rana dalmatina*) that belonged to a species that enjoyed a warm climate.

All this evidence was only the start of the work necessary to support the idea of an interglacial. Processing the critical pollen would take some time, but Rowena Gale was now able to tell us that the pieces of wood near our mammoth tusk were oak (*Quercus*), and the root systems near the *Corbicula* shells were willow or poplar – both associated with moist or, occasionally, flood soils. Dogwood (*Cornus*) and viburnums were also found.

Victor was finally able to draw up a picture of Stanton Harcourt's landscape of 200,000 years ago, and the computer team drew together all the data to create a three-dimensional model of the site.

The trench created by the digger had exposed areas of darker material and clays that should correspond to the river channels. The odd bison and horse bone had been uncovered, but nothing major seemed to have been damaged. Our final act was to lift, from our initial trench, the bison skull and the mammoth tusk, which turned out to be about 3 m (6 ft) long. Kate was confident that the digger trench would give her new areas of rich deposits to work on in the time she had left. Stanton will soon become a waste tip, but at least some of its secrets have been revealed – and saved.

Final thoughts from Mick

I was always sure that Stanton Harcourt would be an environmental archaeology exercise. While further excavation would undoubtedly prove useful, it was always going to be a long shot, hoping to find further hand-axes or other evidence of people.

However, with the best experts, we could create a very detailed picture of what the area looked like in this remote period of the past. It was fascinating to see Russell and Mike convert samples of mud into meaningful descriptions of the landscape, and then see Victor create images of how these might have appeared to the inhabitants back then.

In the end, it did not matter that we did not find any axes – we could imagine what the countryside, through which our ancestors hunted, looked like.

Some of the Palaeolithic bones, teeth and tusks found at Stanton Harcourt. *(Mick Aston)*

TEMPLECOMBE

SOMERSET

WHAT MIGHT HAVE HAPPENED

For the old knight – and the family who had paid for it – the new preceptory chapel floor was a great source of pleasure. The craftsmen had done a good job, with the family's coat-of-arms etched into each tile. The potters' work had gone well, too: the creamy-white slip had filled each shape to perfection, and the final glaze was lustrous enough to reflect the afternoon sun. Although the last few years had been fraught with difficulty – the new intake of Knights Templar didn't seem to adhere to the rules like in the old days – the new floor was still something to be proud of, showing that at least some people respected their Order.

As he gazed across to the hills and to Shaftesbury beyond, the knight could see at the edge of the fields the old wall that defined the limits of the Order's land as well as the limits of the Crown's ability to levy the taxes that were proving so onerous for the villagers. Almost seven feet high, the wall's narrow profile had withstood the course of time well. Soon services would be held in the new chapel, and on those special occasions, the public would be welcomed into the preceptory's precincts. The knight could still remember the less well-publicised rituals that were the darkest secrets of his Order and which bound him and his fellow Templars together – there was talk that some of the brethren had, in the past, worshipped before strange images – but the controversy surrounding the Order meant that many of the glories and mysteries of the past were fading from memory. Still the knight had the warm fire and the thought of the new chapel floor to comfort him...

(Opposite) The strange 13th-century head of Christ in the church at Templecombe. *(Chris Chapman)*
(Above) Victor's version of the austere costume of a Knight Templar.

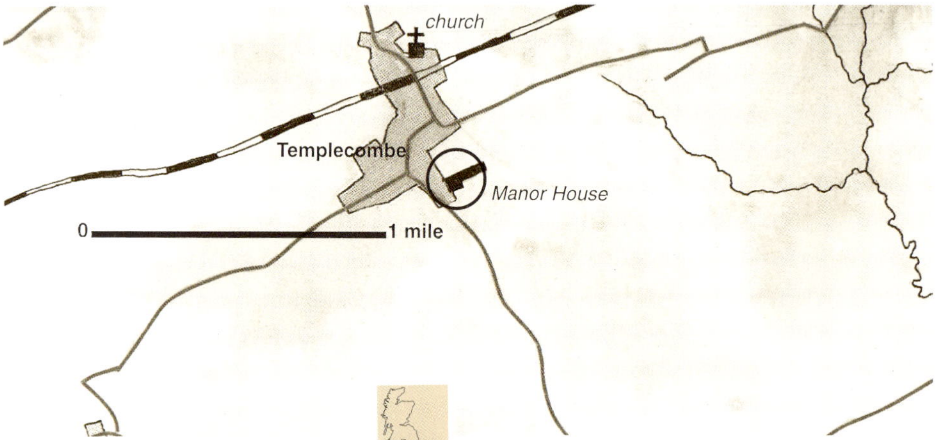

WHY WE WENT THERE

We had been invited to Templecombe in Somerset by Geoff Wilson, the owner of Templecombe Manor. He and his neighbour Richard Hunt, the owner of Manor Farm, occupy much of the land that, history tells us, formed the only preceptory in Somerset built and lived in by the Knights Templar.

At the time of their suppression, which began in 1307, the Knights Templar – or the Order of Poor Knights of Christ and of the Temple of Solomon, to give them their official name – were one of the most powerful forces in Europe: their representatives stood beside kings at coronations, and through their banking activities, they had most of the Royal families of Europe in their debt.

Founded in Jerusalem in 1119, they began as an organisation dedicated to protecting and supporting pilgrims en route to the Holy Land, combining the qualities of devout monks (dedicated to a life closely associated with the disciplines of the Cistercians) and highly skilled soldiers. The backbone of the organisation and defence of the Holy Land, they were known for their great bravery and piousness. They were respected by the Muslims and, in turn, the Templars were able to acquire many skills from their traditional enemies. There is some evidence that, from their foes, they may have learned secrets of navigation and medicine, including the use of a crude form of antibiotic.

This mixture of pious religious observance and military adventure attracted many young men who were not best placed to inherit from their families. The Knights' main source of wealth was, initially, the many small estates and lands granted them by those wishing to enter their number or by those grateful for their protection during a pilgrimage to Jerusalem. As well as defending the latter, the Knights provided them with fresh horses and medical assistance, and they developed an early version of travellers' cheques to help those pilgrims unwilling to carry large amounts of cash. From these small beginnings, the Order gradually became Europe's bankers.

The Knights Templar's affairs were organised around preceptories, which acted as administrative centres. These were often a mixture of farm, bank, hotel and church – a sort of ecclesiastical service station. Within each preceptory were often four to five knights, as well as sergeants, chaplains and servants, all living under strict religious rule, with vows of poverty, obedience and chastity. Prayers were said throughout the day, and the knights were forbidden to wear ornaments and other finery. They were allowed to eat meat on only three days a week, although there is evidence that, as in all medieval homes, ale was the usual beverage, being the only commonly available liquid that was also fit to drink.

From the records, we know that, from 1185 to 1308, there was a preceptory at Templecombe comprising over 400 acres: when the Order was suppressed in 1307, William Raven of Templecombe was the first Templar to be summoned to the Tower for questioning. As well as Geoff's magnificent home, the Sites and Monuments Record (the record of all the known archaeological sites, etc. within a county) also refers to possible fishponds and the existence of a medieval chapel that may have been destroyed when a new house was built at Manor Farm by predecessors of Richard Hunt's family.

We know relatively little about the plans of the Knights Templar's preceptories. The one at South Witham in Lincolnshire, dug by Phil Mayes in 1965–66, is the only example to have been excavated thoroughly. Considering that the Templecombe preceptory was to be our main focus, this gave us little to go on.

Day One

When we arrived at Templecombe, there were two obvious points to start from. The first, Templecombe Manor, appeared to have a basically 17th-century exterior, but both Geoff Wilson and Beric Morley, our buildings expert, felt optimistic that the structure could have been built on earlier foundations. The second starting point was the boundary, which all preceptories created between themselves and the local communities. On an earlier visit,

The first trench on the presumed northern boundary of the preceptory. *(Mick Aston)*

Mick had noticed a fairly clear bank-and-ditch to the south of the modern farm. This looked to be in the right place topographically, appearing to surround the top of the high ground. To the north, a similar steep embankment appeared to perform a similar function.

To locate this northern boundary, we began with a trench, which by the end of three hours of digging had been extended up to the wall of the modern farm garden. Locals had told us that this wall and a ramshackle building next to it had been part of the Templar chapel. We began to locate large amounts of tile debris, some still bearing clear designs. Mick described these as encaustic tiles, and they were obviously from an early chapel. We were able to identify the coat-of-arms on some of them as belonging to Robert Wyvill, Bishop of Salisbury (1330–1375). Such coats-of-arms can be useful indicators for dating buildings. However, it is worth noting that the stamps that made the coats-of-arms were often reused, so the dates cannot be considered definitive.

As the trench was extended, we began to find larger stones embedded in the base of the garden wall. By comparing these with some early photographs, it became clear that the stones were indeed the footings of the Templar chapel. We did not, however, have any clear indication of anything that could be called a boundary ditch or wall. Had this been removed?

Two other questions were raised by the end of the day: did the remains of the chapel continue under the wall and beneath the later building, and did it link up with Geoff's home? Inside the manor house, Beric had identified two or three parts that could have been earlier than the rest of the building. For example, a massive kitchen range with two huge cross beams had caught his eye. Unfortunately, these beams turned out to be elm, which cannot be dated by dendrochronology. However, above the range was an oak beam of about the same length, and this, if we were lucky, might produce a date.

We resolved to look into the farmer's strawberry patch located inside the remains of the stone building at the end of the garden, to see if the chapel walls or floor extended towards Geoff's home. The most pressing problem, and one that would have to be addressed the next day, was the lack of a boundary. Topographically, both the first trench and a second placed to the south, in a paddock adjacent to the farm, should have been where one would expect to find a wall or a bank-and-ditch. As it turned out, the southern trench revealed only an accumulation of shell-like material probably created by the plough line. However, geophysics seemed to have found other anomalies in that area, and it was resolved to explore those early the next day.

Day Two

After a morning's excavation, a large piece of masonry appeared out of the strawberry patch. This stone, the size of a small grave slab, was big enough to have been part of a building, but it was at a higher level than the stone footings we had discovered the previous day, which we knew to be Templar. In

Dendrochronology

This is a relatively recent method of giving quite precise dates for archaeolo-gical sites where wood has survived. It is based on the idea that the growth rings of trees – only oak has been studied so far – vary from year to year according to weather conditions, and that patterns of greater and lesser growth can be compared from tree to tree and from area to area. By working backwards from surviving trees, from timbers in old houses and in even earlier churches, and from wood from excavated sites. a 'master chronology' has been built up. Any timber discovered in buildings or in waterlogged deposits can then be compared with the growth rings already known. If the outer rings of the tree or the sapwood are present, a very precise date can be suggested for when the tree was felled. As most wood in the past seems to have been worked and used 'green', such a date will be very close to that of the construction of the feature under investigation.

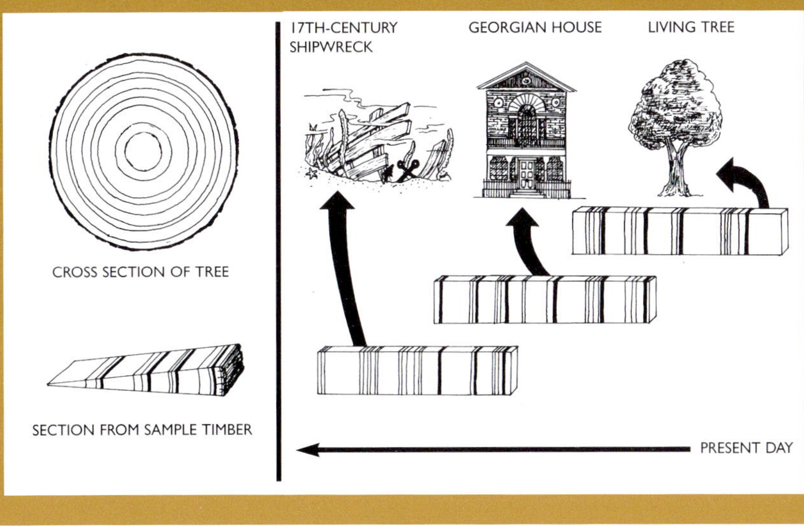

The kitchen range in Templecombe Manor. The dendrochronological sample was taken from the oak cross beam just above the deer's head. *(Mick Aston)*

the paddock, those digging in the second trench again found nothing medieval – the geophysics anomalies had turned out to come from a modern land drain.

It was at this stage that a sense of frustration began to set in, and the team decided to review all the evidence they had accumulated – much of it negative. This included the disappointing result from the dendrochronology, which gave a date of 1610–15 for the oak beam that was part of the manor-house kitchen range. Mick and Carenza decided to look through all our documents to see if we had missed anything.

This gave Robin a chance to catch up on Templar history. As usual, he had been working through the documents and, with Victor, had created an image of a typical Templar knight. The Templars were much less grand than our romantic image of medieval knights – they had to adhere to a rule that demanded an austere appearance. The Order's great power was partly due to the exemptions and rights granted them by the papacy (the Order had been placed under direct papal authority by Innocent II in 1139). They could absolve fellow members, and this allowed them to avoid excommunication and so be independent of any bishops who might wish to control them. Their international links helped immensely in their financial dealings, which took on increasing importance throughout the 13th century as the Crusader states in the Holy Land declined. (Palestine was ultimately lost to Christendom in 1291.)

Ultimately the Knights overstretched themselves and were attacked by the French king, Philip IV, who like many other European rulers owed the Templars money. He persuaded the Avignon Pope Clement V that the Order's power had to be curtailed. On Friday, 3 October 1307, Templars throughout France were arrested. They were accused of a variety of reputedly vile crimes, including spitting on the cross, worship of strange idols and homosexuality, and under torture, many confessed. In England, the newly crowned Edward II was unconvinced by these accusations and dealt leniently with the Order until the Pope insisted. Members of the Inquisition arrived to do their worst, but the English to their credit failed to cooperate and only two Templars – out of a total of 144 in the Order in England – were ever tortured, without result. Clement V did, however, force the closure of the Order in April 1312, and the Templars were doomed to extinction.

It is recorded that three Knights from Templecombe spent some time in the Tower – William de Burton, John de Aley and Walter de Rokele. As with those of the rest of the Templars, their properties were passed on in many cases to another military religious Order: the Knights Hospitaller of St John of Jerusalem, which have continued to follow something like the Templar path. Today there are still 8000 Knights Hospitaller, with their headquarters in Rome, and the next time you attend a football match or village fête, reflect on the ancient origins of the St John Ambulance, who carry on a proud tradition.

A footnote to the story of the Templar's rumoured secret rites is provided by a strange image hanging in the church at Templecombe. This appears to be a portrait of Christ's head that, in some respects, resembles the image on the Turin Shroud. It has two remarkable and – from a medieval Christian point of view – disturbing features: the head is cut off at the neck and there is no halo. This painting came to light in this century when a storm damaged an outbuilding. The picture has been dated to the early 13th century, and it clearly corresponds to one of those images that the Templars were accused of worshipping. It still retains a strange power, and its lack of conventional Christian form implies at least an element of idolatry – and perhaps something darker ...

Day Three

First thing in the morning, distinctly impious noises were coming from Mick Aston's vicinity as he began to realise that we had overlooked a vital clue in our analysis of the site. As an Order of the Church, the Templars would have been exempt from paying taxes, and in some cases, tithe maps still retain a record of medieval tithe-free land. We had the relevant tithe maps, but a bit of detailed work was needed to highlight the land owned by the Templars. Once this had been done, it became clear exactly which fields had been within the preceptory and that these were to the *north* of the modern farm, not the south. By not checking what Mick regards as one of the most basic pieces of archaeological evidence – the tithe map – we had effectively wasted two days of work.

Only our first trench had been placed in a useful position. Trench two

The strawberry patch excavation, protected by an air tent. The medieval walls excavated are clearly visible. *(Mick Aston)*

in the south field, and a third trench begun in the same location towards the end of the previous day, had produced nothing of interest because they were outside the main area of Templar buildings. Beric's work had become equally frustrating. The focus of the main area on the map appeared to be away from Geoff's kitchen range, which may explain why we were failing to find clear evidence of Templar foundations there. And despite the use of remote cameras to look behind walls and under floors, few of the features of the manor house, many of which were of great architectural interest, appeared to be from the 13th or 14th century. Only a plentiful supply of Phil's home-made beer enabled us to keep our spirits up – I can recommend the vanilla flavour!

In the limited time left, it was decided to get John to search the northern fields for possible boundaries. Mick was initially reluctant to open up a fourth trench, but John and the geophysics team worked wonders and in double-quick time came up with what we thought might be a good target. A mechanical digger was summoned to remove the surface plough soil to see what lay beneath.

Phil, Carenza and Mick stood by, and when the digger had dug to 23 cm (9 in) of the surface, stonework began to appear. Hand excavations followed, and with only two hours remaining, Phil finally held up a piece of brown crumbly pot and pronounced it medieval. This gave us an approximate date for the stonework, which made it contemporary with the Templars.

Fate had a final surprise for the team. Carenza decided to wander into an adjoining field to see if the line of stonework appearing in Phil's trench continued. There, covered from sight by undergrowth and a row of shrubs, was the remnants of a wall – of just the right type to indicate a 13th/14th-century origin. The 'clincher', as Carenza put it, was the massive build-up of plough soil behind this wall, indicating many centuries of agricultural activity adjacent to it.

With barely an hour to go, we had at last found our boundary. In the process, we had all learned a lot of lessons and experienced the frustrations and trials that are all part of archaeology. We had not found the actual pieces of Templar architecture that Geoff Wilson had been hoping for. But as Beric Morley pointed out, everybody who had visited the site and had seen the magnificent manor house and the topography of the area around it had assumed that the preceptory would be orientated to the south of the farm.

We had also been prey to what can so easily happen given the three-day time-scale of TIME TEAM: we had followed a false hypothesis and had nearly run out of time to correct ourselves. We had also failed to look at the obvious at an early stage – the tithe map had held all the answers, but we had been distracted by the buildings and topography in front of our eyes. Still, in the end, we did find the boundary, and this means that future planning permission to the north will become much more critical – it is here that the heart of the Templar lands of Templecombe may well be hidden.

Final thoughts from Mick

Finding the Knights Templar preceptory at Templecombe has proved to be a problem over the years. I felt that, given the TIME TEAM resources, we really should at least be able to define its perimeter.

By the beginning of Day Three, I was very angry with myself – if only I had appreciated the map of the tithe-free land earlier, we might have learned much more. However, the situation was not lost, and by the end, using a combination of evidence, we had a good idea of the extent of the Templare establishment – and readers (and viewers) will now know that we make mistakes and misjudgements like everybody else!

(Above left) The 13th/14th-century stone wall discovereed by Carenza Lewis in the north field. *(Mick Aston)*
(Above top) The final stages of work in the top of the long initial trench, with the chapel doorway and other foundations clearly revealed. *(Mick Aston)*

TEIGNMOUTH

DEVON

WHAT MIGHT HAVE HAPPENED

The sailors admired the new cannon. The edges of the shields that embellished their surfaces caught the light as the boat plunged into the tumbling waves, and they gave some comfort, some promise of protection to a crew that was far from home. Opportunities for trade along the coast were good, despite the enmity between the Spanish king and the English queen, but the currents were always treacherous and the easterlies often threatened to blow them past the safe harbours of the River Exe.

Through the spray and the distant gloom, a small group of lights beckoned. The captain ordered the guns primed and demanded more effort from his rowers. The ship's company could not be certain of their welcome, and although the mouth of the river appeared to offer a haven, the coast was notorious for sand bars.

When the oars first struck the sandy bottom in the darkness, the crew began to panic. The ship lurched, and the cannon, which had been their pride, broke loose and smashed into the rails. Water broke through the oarports, and the sailors trapped below deck were smothered by the storm-driven waves that lashed both the ship and the red rocks on the shore.

One of the bronze cannon from the wreck, with the heraldic shields showing clearly. *(Mick Aston)*

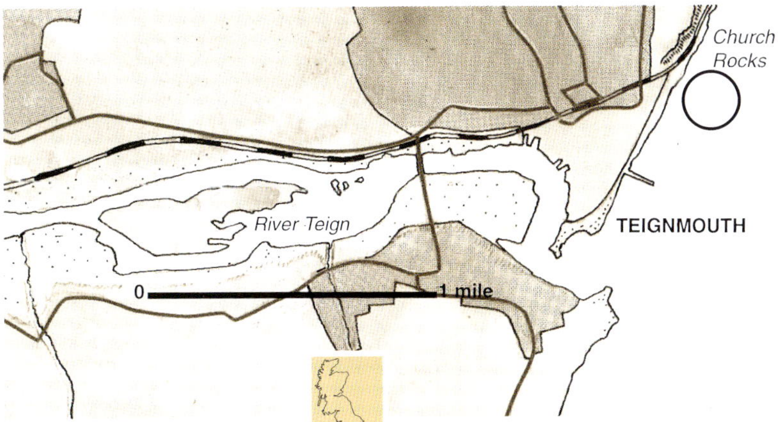

WHY WE WENT THERE

This TIME TEAM adventure began four months before we actually started filming, when Phil and Carenza agreed to go on a diving course (Mick, for health reasons, couldn't join in). Four days of intensive training would allow them to obtain their BSC novice diver's qualification, which in turn would enable them to dive at an underwater site if accompanied by fully trained 'buddies'. Tony already had his qualification, and for some time, we had wanted to do a sub-aqua site. I think we'd all imagined that this would probably be in the blue waters of Greece, but in typical TIME TEAM style, we started our underwater explorations at Teignmouth in Devon!

Anyone who has journeyed down to Devon and Cornwall on the train will have passed the steep red cliffs on the coast at Teignmouth, and our site – Church Rocks – was just 150 m (495 ft) from the railway line itself. Here, in 1975, a 13-year-old spear fisherman called Simon Burton had found a bronze cannon called a 'saker'. Other finds were to follow, and in cooperation with Teignmouth Museum and Historical Society, these were conserved and displayed. The original saker was identified as Venetian, made by the Alberghetti family in the early 17th century. The initials 'SA' that appeared on the cannon suggested that this may have been the work of one of the two Alberghettis called Sigismondo, who had worked in Venice between 1539 and 1684. Analysis of the style of the letters and the design of the decoration narrowed this down to the early part of the second Alberghetti's career, indicating manufacture between 1582 and 1601.

In 1977, the site had been designated a protected wreck (similar to being 'scheduled' on land). At various times, Simon Burton, his father, the late Philip Burton, and a number of local enthusiasts worked on the wreck. However, their resources were limited, and they were aware that seasonal storms could be destroying what was left of the wreck.

An assessment of the wreck site published in 1993 was an attempt to record the work that had been done in the early days, and it clearly showed the need for a thorough, accurate survey of the wreck to assist in its future care and protection. Simon Burton (now 33) had written to TIME TEAM and suggested that we join him, Chris Preece, an underwater archaeologist, and Roger Strudwick, a diver with long-term experience on the site, during their 1995 excavation season.

Day One

Our preparations for the underwater excavation, particularly with two novice divers, required a great deal more time than those for the usual TIME TEAM digs, but by the first morning, the various elements had been assembled and we had established our headquarters in the newly refurbished Royal Teignmouth Yacht Club, which overlooked the site. Out at sea, our diving support vessel was standing by. The *Terschelling*, owned by Nigel Boston, would provide a platform for the divers as well as for the pumps operating the airlifts that would suck away the large amounts of sand that covered the wreck. An airlift works by using a high-pressure pump to introduce air at the mouth of a long tube; as the air bubbles expand inside the tube,

(Above) Close-up of one of the shields on the 'saker' cannon, with the initials 'SA' beneath. *(Mick Aston)*

(Top right) View over the wreck site, with the support ship *Terschelling* on the right and, opposite on the shore, the white-fronted Royal Teignmouth Yacht Club, TIME TEAM's HQ. *(Mick Aston)*

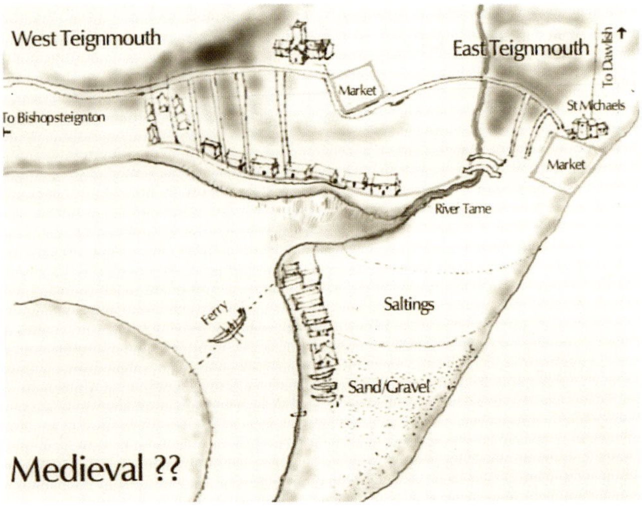

the suction created drags up the sand, to be expelled on the surface. It takes a great deal of expertise to operate air-lifts, and their use has to be carefully monitored in areas where finds may still exist.

As with many other TIME TEAM excavations, our first requirement was to survey the site. Simon's locations for the wreck had been based on estimations, and having no GPS system (*see* p. 8), we could not be certain of exactly where the wreck was.

Carenza and our marine geophysicist, Clive Sawyer, joined the survey vessel that was employing a mixture of sonar and magnetometry to sweep the site. Sonar can, under ideal conditions, penetrate the surface of sand using high-energy, low-frequency sound waves, and this can provide a picture of what may be hidden below. Like all geophysics, it depends on anomalies between the signals reflected by the natural back-ground – in this case, sand and rocks – and those bounced off the man-made objects that we were looking for. As, over the years, Simon and his helpers had brought up a great many finds, including cannon, cannon balls, metal-work and pottery, it was likely that there would not be massive amounts of material left. In addition, the wreck had been made of wood, which, when waterlogged, would not provide a strong signal.

We had hoped that, by the end of the day, we would have a survey that would locate the wreck, but the survey vessel had little to show Carenza and Clive. Had the winter storms removed what was left of the wreck? The lack of survey results meant that we would have to locate it using divers. Chris Preece, the archaeologist who would be in charge of the excavation, was still absent – he was due to return from the Middle East that evening – and as the rules allowing access to sites are very strict, we were not able to enter the wreck area with divers until he arrived.

However, we could continue our investigations on dry land. Robin had begun his research into the shields on the cannon, the coat-of-arms on which had been enigmatically listed as 'unidentified' in all the reports on the wreck. The Teignmouth Museum and Historical Society's report described the shields on one of the cannon as:

Foliated shield enclosing coat of arms (unidentified) of crest of Fleur de Lys and Eagle heads shield with quarterings Dexter, a lion rampant; Sinister upper an unidentified object, Sinister lower, a rose or cartwheel.

After following a false trail that led him to think that this might be a Dutch ship, Robin came to the conclusion that these shields represented a number of Venetian merchants who, over time, had invested in the ship, and therefore an absolute date was impossible to ascertain.

This cannon, which is now at Pendennis Castle near Falmouth in Cornwall, was found to be loaded with iron shot and with the tampion – a wood plug – still in the muzzle. At the time of its original use, it could have fired a 2.7 kg (6 lb) iron ball accurately over 365 m (400 yd) and had a long-range distance of over 1280 m (1400 yd). Later in the weekend, we would have a cannon-firing demonstration and would learn some of its secrets.

Mick had started trying to get an idea of what Teignmouth would have looked like at the time our ship had been wrecked – the late 16th century – and Stuart was working on the changing shape of the estuary itself. It soon became clear that Teignmouth had once been a very different place from the seaside town we see today.

Some of the changes it had under-gone had not been voluntary. Like all ports along the English coast, Teignmouth had been vulnerable to attack, and we knew that the French had all but destroyed the town on 25 July 1690. In addition, the German air force had bombed it during World War II, and recent road schemes had carved up the older town structure.

Mick was by now heavily into what he calls 'regressive map analysis'. This involves assembling as many historic maps of a location as possible and then plotting one on top of the other to see which streets and built-up areas of the modern town correspond to those of an earlier period. The area around Teignmouth's Quay certainly looked old, and according to local historians, one building had survived the French raid – a pub now called The Jolly Sailor. We had asked Beric Morley to investigate this and other buildings to see if any of them would have existed at the time of our wreck. It was also agreed that, if permission could be obtained, a visit to The Jolly Sailor might prove worthwhile.

On board the *Terschelling*, all Phil

Two maps drawn by Victor showing how Teignmouth altered over centuries. *(Left)* An educated guess at what the town looked like in the Middle Ages. *(Right)* The same area as revealed by a map from 1759, showing the narrowing of the River Teign and the growth of the town almost 70 years after the French raid.

could do was prepare his equipment and do a few practice dives. Because of her state of health, Carenza had been advised not to dive, so it would be just Phil and Tony who would be going down first thing in the morning.

When Chris arrived at the end of the day, we were able to tell him about the negative results from the survey. We just had to hope that Simon and Roger could locate the wreck using their own measurements.

Day Two

At last the diving could begin. After an initial recce that located an earlier marker buoy, Chris surveyed an area for excavation and the 'sandsuckers' began their work. This arduous task was only possible with the assistance of a team of support divers from the *Terschelling*.

Phil was now able to get his first experience of underwater archaeology. Added to the strain of coping with the equipment, the most immediate difference from his previous training dives was the state of visibility. The sandsuckers throw up vast amounts of sand, some of which becomes suspended in the water. It's rather like swimming in thick soup, with the visibility at times going below 1 m (3 ft).

On land, Mick temporarily abandoned his maps to be introduced to Nick Hall from the Royal Armouries at Fort Nelson, who would be firing a replica cannon for us. Unlike the saker found on the wreck, this would be a breech-loaded weapon, similar to the three smaller swivel guns found on the site in 1977. One of these had been recovered with swivel and breech block intact. These guns, probably made in *c.* 1580 by the Alberghetti family, were covered in 'sun god' and 'angel' motifs. Loaded with chain shot that was devastating at close quarters, and mounted on the ship's rails, they would have been used to attack opposing crews. The advantage of breech loading is the increase in speed of fire: the breech blocks that hold the powder could be prepared in advance and quickly placed in the weapon.

The astonishing aspect of the cannon firing that we witnessed was the noise and force of the explosion. The shock wave created made us realise just what the effect of many such weapons being discharged in a sea battle would have been – for one thing, it may have deafened many of the crew.

Underwater, we had begun to realise that the job of shifting the sand was going to take longer than anyone had estimated. The sand's fluid quality meant that, almost as soon as it was created, a small hole would backfill. The *Terschelling* had provided more air-lifts, but the work was still slow, and although Simon had found a marker that he had previously placed in the wreck site, by the end of the day we still hadn't found a single ship's timber!

We had, however, been able to understand a bit more about the historical context of the site and what kind of ship we were looking for. The general view of both Simon and the Teignmouth Museum and Historical Society is that this wreck may well be a Venetian galley similar to those that once traded with the south coast ports, particularly Southampton. These vessels were crewed by sailors and up to 300 galley slaves. The majority of galleys in the Mediterranean relied on rowing power to back up sail, but it is now thought that this kind of vessel was less well adapted to the heavier seas of the Channel.

There is a chance that our ship may have become involved in some way with the Spanish Armada of 1588. The age of the guns showed that the boat could have been trading at that date, and it is known that such vessels were often seized by the Spanish and used for their own purposes. Teignmouth was fairly close to the Armada route, and there is some evidence of small vessels called *zabras* being wrecked at

(Above) Diving at the wreck site, with the visibility greatly reduced due to the sand excavation.
(Top right) Mick Aston (*left*) and Nick Hall of the Royal Armouries, with the breech-loading cannon. *(Mick Aston)*

that time, which could fit the description of the Church Rocks wreck.

The Armada was an attempted invasion of England spurred on by the religious differences and power struggles of Elizabeth I and Philip II of Spain. By 1587, Philip had seen his dream of reuniting the Catholic powers of Europe destroyed by the Protestant Elizabeth. Not only had she executed the Catholic Mary Queen of Scots in that year, but she had supported the Dutch Protestants in open rebellion against Spain and encouraged her naval forces to harass and attack Philip's main source of income – the gold fleets from the Americas. On 31 May 1588, the Armada consisting of 125 ships set sail to attack England, but a combination of unfavourable weather, quicker and more agile English boats, and failures in Spanish tactics caused it to disintegrate over the months that followed. The Spanish faced a horrendous journey – north up the Channel, around the tip of Scotland and south past Ireland – before they could set a course for home, with storms destroying many boats off the Irish coast.

In the early stages of the hostilities, the Spanish seized passing merchantmen, and it is possible that the Teignmouth wreck was one of these. However, as Mick and Robin pointed out, the wrecks resulting from the Armada are well documented – at that time, England was prepared for invasion and a close watch was kept along the coast. The cannon found at Church Rocks would have been a valuable commodity, and it seems unlikely that a ship would have gone down with such 'attractive pickings', as Robin put it, without being noticed by the locals. However, there are no contemporary references to a shipwreck – including no records of burials – hence Robin's suggestion that the boat may have been wrecked at night in a bad storm some time before or after the Armada, when coastal observation of passing craft had ceased to be so important.

The other clue we had to the ship's likely history was Venice. From the 14th to the 16th century, Venice was the major seapower in Europe, and acted as the maritime bridge between the Christian empires of Europe and the nations of the Middle East and beyond. The Venetians' skill in navigation and boat-building, when combined with an increasing world market, resulted in the creation of a massive fleet and, because all goods carried were taxed, a rich trading empire. The trading contacts that Venetian vessels maintained were in part represented by some of the artefacts found already at Church Rocks. As well as the Venetian bronze cannon, there was majolica pottery and

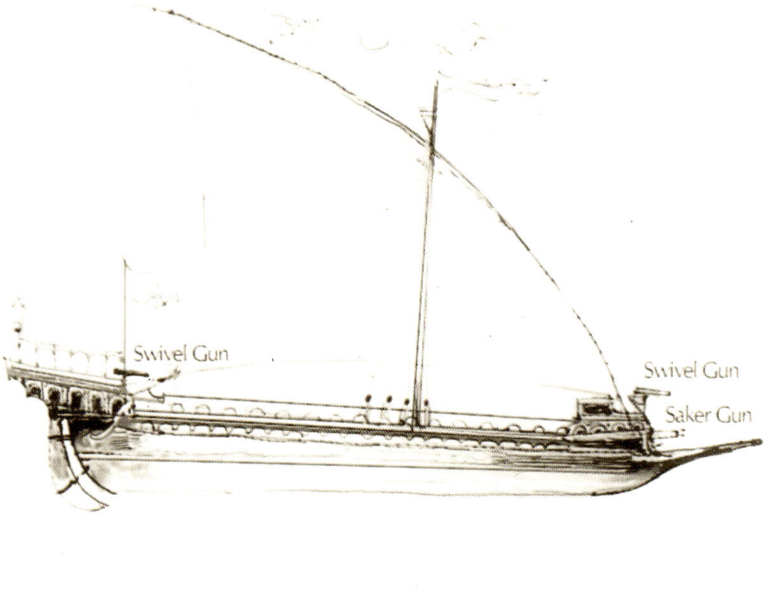

(Top) The galleons of the Spanish Armada of 1588 encounter the agile English ships. *(Mary Evans Picture Library)*
(Above left) Victor's reconstruction of the Venetian galley sunk at Church Rocks, showing the position of the guns and cannon found at the wreck.
(Above right) The 'firepot' found at the wreck site and now at Teignmouth Museum. *(Mick Aston)*

a firepot (an early form of hand grenade) from Spain and sherds of Wan-Li Chinese porcelain dated 1560–1600.

We had as yet found no such evidence ourselves, and by the end of that day, we would have been happy to find anything that could show that the ship still existed. Despite the removal of about 1.2 m (4 ft) of sand, no signs of timbers or artefacts had appeared. A liberal toast of ship's rum was needed to maintain our optimism!

Day Three

Our luck finally changed: we at last found the edge of a wooden beam that Simon identified as part of the wreck. Studding the surface were the corroded forms of 'ghost nails' – concretised shapes that were created around the original nails.

We had also finally arranged to explore inside The Jolly Sailor, where Mick and Beric were able to look at the roof timbers. Since people began living in buildings, the art of the carpenter and his ability to structure timber has been critical. Wood flexes and moves over time, responding to heat, cold and humidity. Structures made from bits of wood simply nailed together quickly break apart – for example, nails hammered into oak rot due to the acidic nature of the tannin in the wood – so a key element of the carpenter's trade was his ability to create strong joints that would attach one piece of a structure to another but also allow some flexing. In its lifetime, a building will not only have to deal with the weight of its own structure, but also the weight of the owners' possessions within it and the effect of wind on the outside.

Early wooden structures were often simply built of logs notched into one another, but the increasing scarcity of lumber increased the pressure to construct houses using only wooden frameworks. The joints in these framework houses have changed over time, but it has not been a simple chronological development, since different joints have occasionally fallen out of use only to reappear at a later stage. However, enough good examples still exist to enable archaeologists to develop a typology of joints (*see* p. 14) that can help them to date other structures. In Britain, the work of the late Cecil Hewett remains the major authority on timber structures.

At The Jolly Sailor, Beric identified a 'notched lap joint', which he said was about the only strong joint used in the 12th and 13th centuries for this kind of structure, but in the West Country, it had enjoyed a revival in the late 16th and early 17th century. In general, the pub's roof lacked any of the features of the 18th century (when Teignmouth was substantially rebuilt), and Beric described it as 'sub-medieval' in appearance. The notched lap joint and the general structure of the building enabled him to date The Jolly Sailor to before the French raid of 1690 and, therefore, contemporary with our wreck.

Back at the wreck site, part of an even more substantial timber was appearing before our eyes. Over 3 m (10 ft) of planking had now been revealed (eventually over 6 m/20 ft would be seen). Tony was able to swim the length of the timber and report that it appeared to continue down into the sand. Because it had part of the stern post attached, Sue and Steve, our graphics team, were able to show where it would have been on the ship before the wreck.

Teignmouth proved to be a major challenge for TIME TEAM, and we were now a lot more aware of the problems of underwater archaeology than when we began. The time needed to remove the sand had taken us by surprise – as Chris Preece said, everything below water takes three times longer than it does on land. However, we were lucky in having an excellent team of support divers and crew to help us, and this made us feel much more positive about trying another diving site in the future.

Phil assured us that he would never again complain about digging in muddy trenches with poor visibility in wet weather! He also said that seeing the timber had been a magical moment, appearing as it did just when we had begun to think that the storms had removed the Church Rocks wreck for ever. Still, that's TIME TEAM for you!

Final thoughts from Mick

I had mixed feelings about Teignmouth. It was easy to feel out of the 'main' action as I was not diving due to recurring chest trouble, so we busied ourselves on shore. The wreck was exciting, of course, and further studies of the remains and its contents will be necessary, but Beric's work at The Jolly Sailor was of great interest, and I would not have missed the cannon firing for anything! To stand next to it as the gunpowder exploded taught me in a few seconds more about fighting at sea in earlier times than all the books put together.

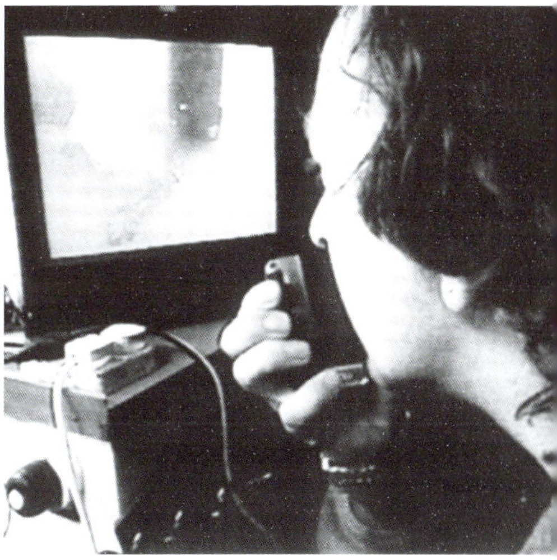

(Left) A 'ghost nail' in a piece of timber taken from the wreck. *(Mick Aston)*
(Right) Tony Robinson speaking to one of the divers while watching the underwater work on closed-circuit television.

NAVAN

COUNTY ARMAGH

WHAT MIGHT HAVE HAPPENED

The hills had been sacred since the times of the ancestors and celebrated in the legends of the ancient ones. The monk knew that to place such a settlement here would be to join a long line of worship – even if, in the past, this had not always been Christian. The people believed in the power of the place, and that the pools and groves hidden below the hills contained ancient memories of the long dead; sparkling treasures and darker secrets of human sacrifice remained part of their folk tales. Ancient pathways still connected the landscape, and each hill's name spoke of the secrets of the Táin *– the stories that no amount of biblical sermons could wrest from the people's minds.*

As he bent his head to catch the final rays of the sun that illuminated the hills of Navan, the monk wrote down the names of each and the palace that the people believed had once capped it. Perhaps the settlement's own modest stones would find a place in the people's stories and spread the light that Patrick had brought to Armagh.

(Above) Aerial photograph showing the mound and ditches that are the only visible remains at Navan today. *(Mick Aston)*
(Opposite) Looking up towards the top of Navan. *(Mick Aston)*

WHY WE WENT THERE

The practice of searching ancient literature for clues to archaeological sites has had a somewhat chequered history. To imagine that legends written at the dawn of history might contain elements of objective fact and description of use to archaeologists takes something of a leap of faith, but there are some cases where this has produced spectacular results.

Around 1870, the wealthy German Heinrich Schliemann became convinced, after examining the details in Homer's *Iliad*, that he could locate the ancient capital of Troy at a site near Hissarlik in Turkey. Subsequent excavation did indeed uncover an ancient city that most archaeologists now accept is the site of Troy. Along the way, Schliemann unearthed some spectacular treasures, including silver and gold objects that he called 'Priam's Treasure', and which, prior to the excavation of Tutankhamen's tomb, were among the most valuable finds ever made.

However, Schliemann's approach alienated many archaeologists at the time and would be regarded as totally unacceptable today. The problem was that Troy was the seventh of nine ancient cities built one on top of the other, and Schliemann disregarded the whole mass of important later historical evidence that lay above it. In his own writings, he refers to the need to 'demolish many interesting ruins in the upper strata'. Despite his destructive methods, Schliemann went on to excavate other sites including Mycenae in Greece, which he referred to as the tomb of Agamemnon – another character from the *Iliad*. Here, again, he uncovered spectacular treasures, although modern archaeologists are less certain about the link with the ancient king.

The great epic of ancient Irish legend is the *Táin Bó Cúailgne* (*The Cattle Raid of Cooley*), and this and the stories of the Ulster Cycle can be seen as the Irish equivalent of the Homeric tales. These legends appear to have been recorded from the 7th to the 14th centuries, but were clearly based on a much earlier oral tradition, and are thought to describe the Celtic world of more than 2000 years ago. The main characters are: Conchobar, the King of Ulster; Cú Chulainn, the heroic warrior; his tutor Fergus mac Roich; Cathbad, the Druid priest; and Deirdre, ward of Conchobar and the Irish equivalent of Homer's Helen. Conchobar's royal palace – and focus of the heroic adventures – was Navan, known in the tales by its Celtic name, Emain Macha.

Emain Macha/Navan was excavated by Dudley Waterman between 1963 and 1971, and a wonderful visitors' centre has since been created. We were invited there by Dr Chris Lynn, Principal Inspector of Monuments, Northern Ireland, to see if we could add some more information about the area around Navan. Chris had asked the question, 'Does Navan stand alone?'

(Top) View of enclosure banks and ditches at Navan. *(Mick Aston)* *(Centre)* Aerial view of the King's Stables, the Bronze Age artificial ritual pool. *(Mick Aston)* *(Above)* Victor's reconstruction of the mouth of the ceremonial trumpet found at Loughnashade.

Cropmarks

These are light and dark marks visible in growing and ripening crops, which reflect differences in the subsoil beneath. As crops, particularly cereals, come to maturity, any parts that are short of water (because they are growing over, say, hidden stone walls or packed stone layers) will tend to grow less and to ripen first, while areas of crops over pits and ditches will tend to remain greener a bit longer and be taller than the rest. However, crop-marks can also be caused by the natural geology of the site, the weather at the time the crop was sown and/or is growing, and numerous other non-archaeological factors.

– the implication being that the whole landscape might be linked together.

The Irish archaeologists already knew of several key sites in the landscape: Navan itself, which now consists of a mound and a number of ditches; the King's Stables, which, despite its name, is a sacrificial pool that had already been shown to contain numerous objects; Loughnashade, where four beautiful ceremonial trumpets were found in the 18th century (three have since been lost, but the remaining one can be seen in the National Museum in Dublin); and Haughey's Fort, a multi-ringed hillfort identified from aerial photographs and the excavations of Jim Mallory from 1988, where an initial geophysical survey suggested another fort structure might exist. Chris was keen to discover if these sites were linked by trackways or ceremonial routes.

The second, somewhat romantic goal for our three days was provided by one of the later Ulster tales, which refers to the existence of *three* palaces at Navan:

> *Three houses had Conchobar, to wit, the Croebruadh [Ruddy Branch], and the Teite Brecc and the Crobderg [Red Branch]. In the Crobderg used to be the heads and spoils, in the Croebruadh were the Kings. In the Teite Brecc there were spears and the shields and the swords.*
>
> Quoted in *Emania* 2 (1987)

None of the tales indicates the precise location of these structures. However, next to Navan is a hill and surrounding area called Creeveroe – or 'Red Branch' – and it was decided that this might be worth looking at. We did have a description of one of the palaces, which was certainly intriguing:

> *Nine compartments were in it from fire to wall. Thirty feet was the height of each bronze front that was in the house. Carvings of red yew therein. A board beneath and roof tiles above. The compartment of Conchobar was in the forefront of the home, with boards of silver with pillars of bronze. Their head-pieces glittering with gold and set with carbuncles ... with its plate of silver above the King to the roof-tree of the King's home.*

Unlike Schliemann, as archaeologists we had certain restraints in dealing with the Navan landscape. The King's Stables is a scheduled ancient monument, and it had to be avoided, and the ancient, vulnerable and important nature of the other sites meant that we had to adopt a careful approach.

Day One

The first morning found us examining a set of ditch features that might be connected with some kind of settlement at Creeveroe. As we were joined by a team of excavators sponsored by the Department of the Enviroment (Northern Ireland) and led by Malachy Conway, Carenza and Chris decided to place our initial excavation across one of these features, and digging commenced.

As often happens with TIME TEAM, our first real finds of importance took us into a totally unexpected era. Phil's luck appeared to be in, as within three

Neolithic stone axe from Tievebulliagh, found in the Creeveroe excavation. *(Mick Aston)*

hours of work, he and the members of Malachy's team had unearthed a Bronze Age stone axehead. This was from a famous axe quarry at Tievebulliagh in Co. Antrim, north of Belfest, and the type of axe that Phil found is regarded as being among the best examples of the axe-maker's art. Such axeheads are found throughout Ireland and in England, to which they were exported.

The axehead didn't, however, help us with our search for evidence of Bronze Age Creeveroe. The excavation then began to produce a series of finds including slag – associated with iron smelting – that might come from the medieval period, but then Bronze Age 'flat-rimmed ware', coarse domestic pottery used for cooking, appeared near the bottom of the ditch. Were we looking at an early ditch that had been reused and filled in later in its existence?

We examined some interesting crop-marks that seemed to indicate a structure connecting Haughey's Fort and the King's Stables. In addition, John's geophysics survey pointed to a useful location for a second excavation that might show such a link.

Artificial pools designed for ritual purposes, such as that at the King's Stables, are important elements of the Bronze Age archaeology of this area. The building of these monuments would have required a massive labour force, and the pools themselves would have been important foci for whole communities. Quite costly objects were thrown into the pools, and it seems likely that their depositing would have involved some complicated ceremonial ritual, possibly involving a connection with the hillforts that rise above each of these pools. The quality of workmanship and the value of the objects also indicate the importance of such sacrificial activities to the community. To put all that effort into an object and then deliberately throw it into a pool reflects a system of beliefs that is difficult for us to understand. In 1976 at the King's Stables, excavation by Chris Lynn revealed Bronze Age sword moulds, bones and the front of a human skull that had been deliberately sliced off from the rest of the skeleton.

Stuart and Bernard from the Royal Commission had been trying to create a model of the hills and valleys around Navan. Their work – and an examination of the aerial photographs of the region by Carenza – had produced another candidate for a possible palace site. This hill, called Bally Doo, was approximately the same distance from Haughey's Fort as Haughey's Fort was from Navan. While surveying the hilltop, Stuart had also noticed a stone with what appeared to be an ancient carving on its side. Did this point to an earlier settlement? The lines formed a V-shape that Victor interpreted as the hind legs of an animal.

Day Two

After discussing the results of John's survey of Bally Doo, it was decided to excavate what looked like a possible defensive ditch. At this point, we were stretched across two to three miles of Irish landscape.

Phil was introduced to an Irish metalworker who would be showing him how bronze plate was worked. Of all the ancient metals, bronze has a wonderful quality that combines durability – it forms a patina but does not rust – with a softness that allows intricate patterns to be etched on its surface. Phil and the metalworker would be producing a copy of the mouth of the remaining Bronze Age trumpet found at Loughnashade.

Communication with our expert did

(Top right) Victor's reconstruction of the full carving on the inscribed stone discovered by Stuart Ainsworth on the top of Bally Doo. *(Mick Aston)*.
(Above) Aerial view of Loughnashade, a natural ritual pool. *(Mick Aston)*

not go exactly smoothly, due to his refusal to speak English: as an Irish craftsman, he believed that Gaelic was the appropriate language to describe his skills. With help from some of the local people, Phil gradually began to get a grip on the situation, and the bronze plate began to take on a recognisable form.

By now, our first trench was showing a clearer stratigraphy. The layer of later soil containing the iron-working slag could be clearly seen, and pottery of an earlier date was appearing in the bottom of the ditch. Large dark brown sherds of a crumbly texture were our first pieces of evidence contemporary with the tales of Conchobar and Cú Chulainn.

The third trench, at Bally Doo, had also begun to show the edge of what might prove to be a pathway surface that appeared to line up with a possible route from Haughey's Fort to the King's Stables. The pottery and this discovery put us in good spirits, and the day ended with a celebration with plenty of Guinness and entertainment by local musicians. The sight of Phil and Robin dancing with the locals was a remarkable one, and Phil's exertions on the dance floor certainly helped to cheer him up after a somewhat frustrating day trying to get to grips with bronze-making skills via ancient Gaelic.

Day Three

The day began with the uncovering of new material from Bally Doo, including the discovery of a piece of fragile metalwork that turned out to be a medieval stirrup. The geophysics team had managed to do a concentrated survey of the top of the hill, which had produced the suggestion of structures, and it was decided to extend our excavation into this area. We began to locate the stonework of what Chris and the other Irish archaeologists thought might be an early Christian settlement. Large amounts of souterrain ware (dark bucket-shaped ware associated with underground chambers) – and a shale bracelet found towards the end of the day – suggested the early date, and a glass bead also found towards the end of the day confirmed this view. Chris Lynn told us that only two types of locations were known to make these beads – early ecclesiastical or royal sites.

With hours to spare, the trumpet mouth was completed, and in trench two, between Haughey's Fort and the King's Stables, the excavation team had revealed more of a path surface. A saddle quern and more Bronze Age pottery found there confirmed the date as contemporary with the King's Stables.

Although we had not unearthed a glittering palace, we had, in working with this ancient landscape in a responsible way, begun to get nearer to some of its secrets. It seems likely that the cropmarks and geophysics surveys point to a number of routes and pathways connecting some of the features in the Navan landscape. In addition, it seems that later generations sought to acquire some of the power of the site when they established their Christian settlements in the landscape.

Final thoughts from Mick

Navan was amazing. Archaeologists often talk about landscape archaeology and ritual landscapes, and here was a stunning example, with enclosures scattered across several miles of the countryside, dating to the Bronze Age, Iron Age and early Christian period. In this context, Armagh as the present-day religious capital of Ireland is merely the logical successor to numerous other religious and political foci in this landscape.

Stratigraphy

A 'section' cut through a site – like a layer cake with a slice removed – can give a detailed look at the history of that specific area, from the geology at the bottom, up through the layers that result from construction and occupation, with recutting of ditches, replacement of walls and the like, to the abandonment of the site and, at the top, the formation of soil with turf. The objects, especially pottery and coins, associated with the layers of a section give good evidence of the date of occupation on the site.

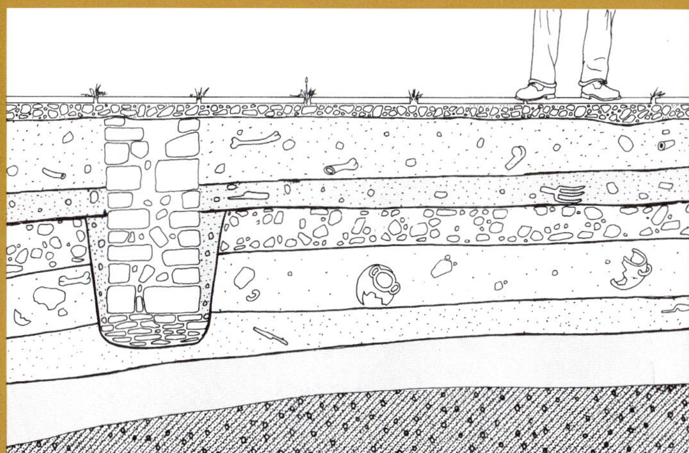

(Top left) The medieval stirrup found at Bally Doo. *(Mick Aston)*.

LAVENHAM

SUFFOLK

WHAT MIGHT HAVE HAPPENED

The regional governor had moved them in as quickly as could decently be done. The legions had hacked the heart out of the rebels, followers of the woman who had dared to attack the Empire, and now those families who had stayed loyal could take their places. Fields and paths were created on a more fitting Roman plan. Two roads were built, and some new workshops were set up to take advantage of the free fuel from the thick forests that surrounded them. Pots and brooches would be produced there. With peace now established, there was a market for their goods – money may be scarce, but their brooches, which had never been expensive, sold well. Bronze tinned with silver plate gave the appearance of sparkle without the cost.

New houses were built and new families moved in. There were a few problems with some of the less scrupulous traders, one among their number attempting to use his brooch-making skills to create false silver coins. The local tax collector demanded his payment in silver but did not always take care to check the piles of coins paid in.

Victor's reconstruction of a typical Roman dwelling in Suffolk.

WHY WE WENT THERE

By English standards, the farms of Suffolk are huge – 500 acres plus is common – and the land they occupy was one of the busiest areas of Roman Britain. However, the increase in intensive agriculture in modern times has meant that, while many small scatters of Roman finds are present here, the sites of the settlements where these objects originated have often been obliterated.

For many years before the Roman invasion of Britain in AD 43, some of the Iron Age tribes of the region – such as the Iceni, the Catuvellauni, and the Trinovantes (first mentioned by Julius Caesar in 54 BC) – traded with Gaul: in his writings, the Roman historian Tacitus (c. AD 55–120) compliments the inhabitants of south-eastern Britain for their readiness to learn Latin. From c. AD 5, the Catuvellauni were ruled by Cunobelin – the historical basis for Shakespeare's Cymbeline – who joined together his tribe and the Trinovantes and created the settlement of Colchester (now in Essex) as a regional capital of Iron Age south-east England. When he died in AD 41, the joint kingdom was divided between his two sons Tigodunnus and Caratacus who reigned for only two years before the invasion led by the Emperor Claudius. On entering Colchester (which the Romans renamed Camulodunum), Claudius was met by a number of tribal chiefs, including those of the Iceni, who were willing to submit to Roman rule. The Catuvellauni and the Trinovantes were treated as defeated enemies, and Caratacus became leader of the British resistance to the conquerors.

TIME TEAM had been invited to Priory Farm near Lavenham, Suffolk by the owner Adrian Thorpe who over the years had, following his keen interest in archaeology, accumulated a vast number of Roman pottery sherds, bits of metalwork and other remains from one particular field on his land, known as 'Old Ley'. Looking at aerial photographs of the farm, this field stands out: it is almost square and much smaller than the fields surrounding it. The photographss also revealed an interesting set of cropmarks that might indicate buildings below the surface. In addition, Adrian had never had a geophysical survey carried out on his land.

TIME TEAM decided to see if a Roman building was the source for all the material that Adrian had collected. The interesting point about Adrian's finds was that they were almost all Roman. Two late Iron Age coins indicated a settlement prior to AD 43, but the rest suggested a village or farm that had flourished in the Roman period and then disappeared from the

Aerial photograph of 'Old Ley', the small, square field in the centre. *(Mick Aston)*

Postholes

Many early buildings and other structures were made of wood, and before the use of stone foundations, their main supports were usually posts set in the ground. To construct these, a hole was dug, the timber was set in, then the hole was filled with a packing of stone or earth. From these holes and the packing around them, archaeologists can recognise sitings of such posts and therefore of the building or structure they once supported, even when the posts have rotted or were removed.

later historical record.

One of Adrian's objects caught Tony's eye – part of a large key. This gave us the main goal for our three days' work: could we find the building that had, in Roman times, contained a door opened by that key?

Day One

'Old Ley' would be our main focus for the weekend, and we asked John to begin early to see if there were any geophysical responses in the areas of the field that corresponded with the cropmarks. However, his results seemed to have only a tenuous link with the marks, and it began to be clear that we were dealing with a site where different periods of occupation had left their own individual patterns of ditches, hedges and, possibly, structures on the landscape.

Our first excavation set out to test the geophysical results, but the trench was also placed near the area of most intensive cropmarks. We located some ditches but nothing that could be considered a building. As Mick pointed out, we were dealing with a period and an area where archaeology is often a question of analysing stains in the ground and the faint signs of postholes and shallow foundations that once formed the main structural components of wooden buildings. We did find some scatters of later Roman pottery but not in a strong enough concentration to suggest that we were adjacent to a building.

By now we had been joined by two metal detectorists, Alan Smith and Terry Marsh, who had established a good reputation with the Suffolk Archaeological Unit. They would be helping us by scanning over the soil heaps created by excavation, looking for any artefacts that may have been missed, and doing some initial sweeps across the surrounding fields. Detectorists are considered by many archaeologists to be a threat to our heritage. Mick refers to them as the 'ram-raiders of the archaeological world' – if a field has been, as he puts it, 'hoovered clean' by detectorists, we may lose vital evidence. This negative attitude has been encouraged by two particular activities that the relatively few 'cowboy' detectorists indulge in. The first is straightforward theft, where they trespass on private land and steal anything they find. The second is that, even when they do have permission to detect on private land, they fail to record the locations of their finds adequately or give maps of them to local archaeologists.

One of the other difficulties in getting the two sides to work happily together is the archaeologists' attitude towards what they call 'unstratified objects'. When a detectorist hears a signal, he or she simply digs the object out of the soil. Archaeologists then have no way of knowing where in the sequence of historical layers that object came from, or if it was accompanied by other material that may help to date or identify it. Scatters of material and their relative concentration may be the only clues we have to the location of some key archaeological sites. If those objects have also been taken out of their context, we may also lose the ability to put together the fragile jigsaw of evidence that enables another archaeological fact to come to light. Detectorists often insist that they only operate in the plough soil layer, where agricultural activity has already spread and possibly damaged objects, but if finds are not mapped, we may still lose valuable archaeological evidence.

Just one coin can alter radically our view of the past of a site. At Lavenham, we had only two pre-Roman coins, but these were enough, along with a few pottery sherds, to provide vital clues

View over the extension of trench one, where dark marks indicated building foundations. *(Mick Aston)*

about the farm's early history. If those coins had ended up in someone's private collection with no record made, we would have known a lot less about the site.

So detectorists with sense and integrity get permission to investigate land, map their finds and give that record to the local museum or archaeological unit. Detectorists who establish a good reputation will often have the chance of working with the local unit and have the satisfaction of knowing that they have contributed to the historical record.

It was fascinating to watch how our two detectorists worked. Most metal detectors can differentiate between ferrous (iron-containing) and non-ferrous material. Because farm fields are usually cluttered with old nails, bits of machinery and so on, it is usual to sweep them on a non-ferrous setting. On a Roman site, bronze and silver coins and parts of brooches and pins will be the usual target. As its head sweeps across an object, the detector bleeps. Because the machine will sometimes give a response to a piece of iron even though in non-ferrous mode, the detectorist will then flick the switch to ferrous mode. If a louder bleep now results, this confirms that it is an iron object and therefore probably of little interest. If the bleep remains faint, the object may be worth digging up.

You have to walk alongside a detectorist for a while to understand how engrossing this activity can be. It must be – after all, endless bleeps and hours of arm-aching work can result only in a few bits of worthless scrap.

However, on an earlier visit to this site, Terry had located a tiny piece of bronze brooch coated with silver. He had marked the spot on his map, including the approximate depth, and had placed the find in a marked bag to be passed on to the archaeologists. And during the TIME TEAM excavations, he and Alan found more brooches and some silver coins.

Day Two

As the day progressed, the geophysics team, who had increased the range of their survey, located what John described as 'areas of intense activity' in three or four locations in 'Old Ley'. It was decided that a new trench should be placed in the vicinity of one of these. A small area of strong magnetic anomalies can be produced by a hearth – fire increases the magnetism of the stones. A find such as this, particularly where structures with little stone in their foundations are suspected, can provide a valuable clue to the location of a building.

Geophysics had also located another area of strong signals not far from our first trench. When a member of the Royal Commission survey team pointed out that these anomalies appeared to create an outline of a building, it was decided to widen trench one, once the initial ditches found had been cleared, drawn and photographed.

As soon as the top soil was removed in trench two, there were clear signs of red rubble and pottery sherds, which indicated that this was not just another ditch. Large pieces of sherds were exposed, and the earth around appeared to have been baked by fire. Could some kind of industrial activity been carried out here, such as a small kiln?

During the day, we began to see the results of this programme's example of historical reconstruction: a working Romano-British glass kiln. Gilbert Burroughes, a local farmer and potter, had agreed to help us by constructing the kiln from slabs of clay that he had pre-fired.

There is no evidence that the Romans actually produced glass in Britain. What they appear to have done is reworked glass from recycled scrap and from raw glass imported from the Continent. The critical difference between making glass and reworking it lies in the construction of the kiln and the temperature needed to heat the glass. To achieve the magical act of transforming sand into glass, you need a substantial temperature of over 1400°C (2550°F). Melting scrap glass requires a lower temperature – about 1200°C (2190°F) – and kiln construction is not as critical. However, because we had decided not to use any modern ceramic materials, achieving the right temperature would not be easy.

John Shepherd of the University of London had agreed to bring us two litres of broken glass that had been found in a Roman glass dump in London. An expert in glass furnaces, he regarded the building and firing of our

(Top left) Terry Marsh scanning one of the excavation trenches. *(Mick Aston)*
(Above) Excavating the square pit in Walnut Tree Field, which was discovered because of a strong geophysical anomaly. *(Mick Aston)*

kiln as such a unique and important experiment that it was worth sacrificing some genuine Roman glass. Adrian and John were joined by old friends of Phil's – Ed Igglehart and his son. Ed, a self-confessed glass enthusiast, had agreed to attempt glass-blowing as the final act of our experiment.

By the end of the day, Gilbert had created a basic shape with the fire-clay bricks. The combustion of the wood would take place to the side of the main kiln, and bellows would force the hot air into the kiln, within which would sit the crucible that would receive the glass. With a plentiful supply of wood from Adrian and Ed's son pumping the bellows, the inside of the kiln gradually began to change colour. This operation, once begun, had to be sustained until the end, which meant a sleepless Saturday night for the glass-makers. A keg of ale – according to Ed, the standard glass-maker's requirement – was there to keep them going.

We returned at midnight to check their progress. As we headed towards the red-glowing fire in the darkness, John's voice could be heard calling out the temperature from two thermo-couples connected to the kiln. Gilbert, smoke-blackened and red-eyed, was stuffing wood into the firebox while Ed gave words of encouragement.

However, there was a problem. Each time the temperature rose above 1000°C (1830°F), it seemed to stutter and fall back. If Ed opened the kiln to look at the glowing clay crucible, the temperature would reduce to below 900°C (1650°F). At this stage, Gilbert made a critical discovery – the kind that makes this sort of experiment so worthwhile. Peering into the firebox, he noticed that a mass of clinker – a kind of crude opaque glass – had built up at the kiln end and appeared to be blocking the entrance. Using one of his fire-irons, he was able to drag out the glowing mass. It was clear that the natural soda in the wood, the soil at the kiln base and some of the clay had combined to form the clinker, and this had blocked the furnace.

Like someone clearing his throat, the removal of the clinker seemed to breathe new life into the furnace and it raced up to 1200°C (2190°F) and stayed there. There was great relief all round – it was now 1.30 am and Ed could at last place the broken Roman glass in the kiln. Cold glass meeting a hot crucible can cause problems, so Ed had to proceed slowly, a few pieces at a time. We left the glass team clustered around their kiln, John quietly reading out the temperature – '1200, 1250, 1300 ...' – and Ed's son gently pumping the bellows.

Day Three

We were all keen to return to the glass-making to see if the kiln had survived the night. Looking like survivors from a forest fire, Gilbert and his colleagues were weary but triumphant. Despite the collapse of part of the firebox, necessitating on-the-spot emergency repairs, the kiln had survived, and Ed had the first glowing pool of molten glass in the base of the crucible. While he built up the amount necessary to blow a vessel, TIME TEAM had to assess the state of the site's archaeology.

As a last act at the end of the previous day, Phil and a member of the Suffolk Archaeological Unit had decided to extend trench one, and this had at last revealed an area of debris that appeared to be a floor. This was cleaned off and examined closely. Overnight Adrian had helped the process by soaking the soil with a crop sprayer. This had begun to show up dark patches that, once cleaned, turned out to be postholes.

Trench two had begun to produce some really exciting material. The red rubble was, it seemed, a possible kiln, and we had got some large pieces of pottery, described by Jude Plouviez, a Suffolk County Council archaeologist, as a drinking cup or flagon. This pottery dated from the very first occupation of the site, possibly around 50 BC, and showed that there had been small-scale industrial activity on the site from an early period.

Having had some success in following up John's strong anomalies in 'Old Ley', Carenza was interested in what she described as a 'Salisbury Cathedral size' anomaly peak on John's printout for the adjacent Walnut Tree Field. As she and Phil watched, the top soil was carefully removed, and once again, we found the same fired clay and soil that we had discovered in trench two. Excavation proceeded by hand, and we uncovered what appeared to be the top surface of

a square pit with scatters of sherds and a fired lining. This feature was to remain a puzzle throughout the final day. The current view is that it was some kind of industrial pit that had been filled with refuse and then burned. It certainly contained a number of things that would account for the strong geophysical signal, including a large amount of iron.

It was now time to return for the final stage in the glass-making. Ed carefully dipped his long steel pipe into the glass and coated it with a layer of the molten material. With Phil standing by as assistant, he collected a larger amount of glass from the crucible and gently blew into the pipe. For the first time in nearly 2000 years, the Roman glass formed itself into a bubble – the first step in making a vessel. After many trial attempts, we eventually achieved a shape that Ed pronounced himself moderately satisfied with.

Phil attached the glass-tipped punty iron to the shape's base, and the new vessel was snapped off from Ed's pipe. The 'punty' provides a weak glass weld between a piece of waste glass and the main vessel. One part of our kiln that had not worked well was the annealing chamber, which provides the essential transitional hot chamber to prevent the glass vessel from cooling too rapidly. Ed had to improvise with an oil drum full of sawdust: the smouldering waste material helps keep the glass at a warm enough temperature to prevent cracking.

At the extended trench one, we were now able to make out postholes and beam slots, the faint traces of the building that had once stood in Adrian's field in Roman times. Throughout that final afternoon, large amounts of pottery quickly came to light. Silver coins were also found and, interestingly, a fake silver coin with a bronze interior. Along with the numerous small pieces of brooch that were present, this suggested that 'Old Ley' field had once been a small settlement with farms but also kilns and metalworking.

The brooches were not of the highest quality – Tony described them as a 'Christmas cracker' type – and it is possible that, here, a settlement of Romano-British people made a living knocking out cheap decorative metalwork for the booming town of Colchester, and occasionally tried their hand at the odd forgery.

By now Stuart had worked out two field systems, one that was early Romano-British and was possibly related to the pottery we had found in trench two, and another system of a later date that might be have been created after the resettlement of the site following the Boudiccan revolt of AD 61.

One of the British tribes in the region, the Iceni, had been a client kingdom of the Romans. However, on the death of their king Prasutagus, the local Roman in charge decided to exert his power and demanded that the Icenis give up their weapons, to remove any threat while the legions were subduing 'rebels' elsewhere in Britain. When the Iceni refused to comply, Boudicca, Prasutagus's widow, was flogged and her daughters raped. Her revenge was to rock to the core the Roman establishment in Britain. Londinium (London) was razed to the ground and Colchester sacked. Only the return of the legions and the arrival of mercenaries from abroad saved the Romans in Britain, and they took care to teach the Iceni a lesson – all of the tribe's lands and those of their supporters were forfeited. It may be that Lavenham felt the effect of this, with new landowners being imposed after the Romans' reconquest. (According to some records, soldiers were given this land as a reward for defeating Boudicca.) They swept the old boundaries away and created new structures, including, perhaps, a link to the Roman road system, which is suggested by a ridge of land that connects 'Old Ley' to the outside world.

It was now time for our final task – to see if the Roman glass had survived the trauma of being melted, blown and cooled down after 2000 years of waiting. Ed dipped his stick into the sawdust, and – to everyone's relief – out came the glass vessel, smouldering, burnished but complete, and, when polished, the same blue hue of the original material. We had all gained a great deal of respect for our glass team and their Roman predecessors.

Final thoughts from Mick

Our work at the site in Suffolk was, in many ways, very typical of archaeological activities in Britain today. There was little to see on the ground, and the main information came from careful fieldwork – in this case, with the sensible use of metal detectors and geophysics. When we excavated 'Old Ley' field, we saw different coloured stains in the soil indicating pits, ditches, hearths and floors. But such slight and ephemeral evidence is often all we have, and it is the skill of the archaeologists and the careful analysis and study of finds that really produce the story from such unimpressive 'finds'.

However, the glass-blowing was probably one of the most spectacular and impressive experimental archaeological exercises the TIME TEAM is ever likely to carry out!

Phil helps to remove the molten glass from the kiln. *(Mick Aston)*

TIME TEAM
SITE UPDATES

Not only does the work of the TIME TEAM have a value of its own, but it can often spur on others to carry out further archaeological investigation. Here are updates on what has happened at sites explored by the TIME TEAM in the last two series.

SERIES I

Athelney & Wedmore, Somerset

There was no excavation at the protected site at Athelney, but the investigation continues, with a report in the county archaeological journal planned for 1996. Since the programme, the farmer has 'unearthed' a number of artefacts (worked stone, tiles, pottery, etc.) from corners of his attic, and these are to be recorded, drawn and included in another future article.

At Wedmore, a small farm site was excavated but, due to lack of time, this was not included in the broadcast programme. The small evaluation trenches dug on the site, in an area earmarked for housing development, provided useful information on the archaeological context of the site. Permission has now been given for development of the site, and the buildings that will appear here have been designed to protect the stratified archaeological remains (early medieval and possibly some Roman).

Llangorse, Powys

Processing the evidence from every excavation season since 1989 is currently underway, and the TIME TEAM artefacts are still being studied. The shell ring has been conserved, and a preliminary assessment of the slags and metalworking evidence from the crannog has been completed. Every effort is being made to protect Llangorse into the next millennium. 1993 was the final year of work on the crannog, and the rest of the remains have been preserved for future investigation. Cadw, in conjunction with the Brecon Beacons National Park, have commissioned a report from engineers on how the erosion can be stopped in order to keep the site safe.

A bone comb from the site (not a TIME TEAM find) is on display at the National Museum in Cardiff; when the archaeological section there is refurbished, Llangorse will be featured heavily as a unique and important site for Wales. A joint publication by the National Museum and the University of Wales will be produced in due course. The results of the TIME TEAM work will be incorporated and published in full. The log boat constructed by TIME TEAM is on display at the 'Pageant of London' exhibition at Tower Hill.

Much Wenlock, Shropshire

The TIME TEAM investigation in Sheinton Street identified a mid-13th century house with a stone-built high end, or solar, and a timber hall beyond, which may have been built as a guest house for visitors to the nearby priory. Excavation extended past the kitchens and uncovered a rear yard and large medieval cesspit. After the team departed, digging continued, which led to the discovery of a well-preserved cobbled courtyard and drain leading up to the back wall of the medieval hall.

Dendrochronological samples gave more precise dates for the building: AD 1254–1290. One timber sample had nearly 400 rings, showing that the tree from which it came would have been planted at around the time of King Alfred (AD 849–899).

Later that year, building work on the other side of Sheinton Street – preceded by archaeological evaluation – revealed traces of lynchets (field boundaries) that may be Anglo-Saxon. This shows that Sheinton Street formed part of the Norman 'new town' that was built over farmland. Other work in the town – again in advance of redevelopment – revealed plans of two more medieval halls, smaller frontage dwellings and backland occupation. These findings broadly confirm the model of the development of the town that was originally suggested by the TIME TEAM. This work will form the basis of a study of the buildings and archaeology of the whole of Much Wenlock in the near future.

The dendrochronology dates have been published in Vernacular Architecture, *and reports on the archaeology of Much Wenlock are available in the Sites and Monuments Record, Shropshire County Council, Shire Hall, Shrewsbury.*

Ribchester, Lancashire

There have been a number of evaluations and watching briefs in the village since the TIME TEAM excavations. Most of these have been on a small scale, but nearly all of them have produced interesting and signficant archaeology that adds to the overall picture of the village.

Results of the TIME TEAM excavations will form part of a forthcoming monograph by English Heritage on the Ribchester Excavations 1989–90. All the finds will be archived and kept in the Ribchester Museum.

SERIES II

Hylton Castle, Sunderland

The development of the parkland surrounding Hylton Castle is part of a City Challenge scheme run by Sunderland City Leisure, which aims to elevate its status and improve its amenities (including the building of an adventure playground). Since TIME TEAM's work, an earthwork survey of the whole area has been completed, more documentary researches have been carried out, and a design strategy for reconstructing the Elizabethan gardens discovered by TIME TEAM has been produced (the search is now on for money to fund this). More trenches are currently being excavated in a fairly sterile area to the west of the castle in anticipation of the footpaths and flowerbeds being laid out. The castle itself is still in the care of English Heritage, which has carried out some conservation work (on beetle infestations, etc.).

Islay, Western Isles

After the TIME TEAM left, the stone-lined chamber on the top of the mound was investigated further, and was found to contain animal bones, a fine Bronze Age flint arrowhead and a bone disc. The chamber may have been a grave, but no trace of burials was found.

Next to the chamber, archaeologists found a Bronze Age cairn that was 3 m (9.8 ft) wide. These are known to have marked the burial places of important individuals, and there was evidence of a cremation burial here.

The chamber finds will be on display at the Finlaggan Visitor Centre in the summer of 1996.

Lambeth, London

The Museum of London is planning to donate to Lambeth Palace some of the artefacts from the TIME TEAM excavations to put on display for visitors.

Tockenham, Wiltshire

After the TIME TEAM's departure, a local team led by Bryn Walters returned to the site and carried out a small excavation to clarify the apsidal structure in the west wing of the Romano-British villa and to see exactly how much had survived. Using the geophysics grid, they immediately encountered the apse, which appears to be polygonal, with five exterior sides and a semi-circular interior. This had once contained a magnificent mosaic floor constructed of very high-quality tesserae (mosaic pieces), which, unfortunately, had been completely destroyed 800–900 years ago.
The great number of tesserae suggest that the mosaic covered the entire chamber; had it survived, this would have been the third largest mosaic-floored hall in England.

The excavators also found that the villa's foundations had been totally robbed away, except for the very bottom courses of local oolitic stone; the rest was simply backfilled rubble. This confirmed the hypothesis that the walls were robbed out to build the earliest buildings in the village. Very little pottery was found.

Winterbourne, Wiltshire

The report on the TIME TEAM excavations is due to be published in the *Wiltshire Archaeological Magazine* in 1996/97. A proposal for writing up the entire cemetery of about 80 burials has been put forward. The most significant outcome of the excavations has been that the pond barrow – a last-minute discovery – has been scheduled as the 61st example of these rare monuments.

The conserved finds from the cemetery are on view in the Salisbury Museum until 27 January 1996.

RESOURCES

GETTING INVOLVED

If you have enjoyed the TIME TEAM series and booklet and want to become more than just an armchair archaeologist, there are a number of organisations that can provide information, advice and participation. Here are some suggestions.

Council for British Archaeology

Bowes Morrell House,
111 Walmgate, York YO1 2UA
Tel: (01904) 671 417

A first step is to find out what is going on near you – there are local and regional groups all over the country. The best source of information is the CBA, members of which include professional archaeologists, local archaeological societies and museums, and lots of interested amateurs. You can join, too!

The CBA provides information, advice and practical support to assist those who want to become involved in archaeology through fieldwork or by participating in meetings and events. Its regional organisations form a countryside network of archaeo-logists. It also publishes a popular news magazine called *British Archaeology*, which ranges right across the subject – from the Stone Age to the archaeology of the 20th century, from conservation to legislation, and from education to the latest discoveries and new ideas.The magazine contains campaigning editorials, as well as feature articles and reviews by some of the best writers and thinkers in the field.

Young Archaeologists' Club (YAC)

Part of the CBA, the Young Archaeologists' Club – whose president is TIME TEAM's Tony Robinson – is for people who, as well as taking archaeology and the country's heritage seriously, know how to have a good time. YAC members – who are between the ages of 9 and 16 – can take part in club activities through local branches around the country; they can also go on field study holidays and even compete for the 'Young Archaeologist of the Year' award. Each member receives the club's quarterly magazine *Young Archaeologist*, which is packed with news from Britain and correspondents abroad, and gives details of things to do and places to go. To contact the YAC, use the same address as for the CBA.

Current Archaeology

9 Nassington Road
London NW3 2TX
Tel/fax: (0171) 435 7517
e-mail: tsubs@archaeology.compulink.co.uk

With six issues a year, this lively and popular colour magazine provides good coverage of news about recent finds, recently published books and topics of debate. Subscribers also get an extremely useful annual *Directory of British Archaeology*, full of the names and addresses of archaeological organisations. The annual subscription is £12.00; for an extra £4.00, you also get the latest three back issues and the *Directory*. There are special offers for new subscribers.

English Heritage Education Service

429 Oxford Street
London W1R 2HD
Tel: (0171) 973 3442/3

In addition to caring for many monuments, Engish Heritage has a superb Education Service to help teachers (at all levels) make full use of the historic environment. Visits to historic sites are a recommended part of the National Curriculum, and the Education Service offers guidance not only on their historical relevance, but also on the part they can play in subjects as varied as English, maths, science and geography. Educational visits to monuments under the care of English Heritage are free.

Nautical Archaeological Society

Contact: Chris Underwood
19 College Road
HM Naval Base
Portsmouth PO1 3LJ
Tel: (01705) 818 419

Runs a special training course for those with experience of diving who wish to become involved in underwater archaeology.

FURTHER READING

Oxbow Books in Oxford specialise in archaeology and carry an enormous stock of books. They also issue free lists of new publications every few months, and can supply all titles by post. Contact:
Oxbow Books, Park End Place, Oxford OX1 1HN
Tel: (01865) 241 249
Fax: (01865) 794 449

General books

The Time Team Reports by Tim Taylor, Channel 4 Television, £3.50.These are the full site reports for the last series, when the team investigated the Scottish island of Islay, a castle in Sunderland, a Romano-British villa in Wiltshire, the Thames in London, and a Saxon cemetery near Salisbury. To obtain a copy, send a cheque or postal order to: Time Team Reports, PO Box 4000, London W5 2GH.

Interpreting the Landscape: Landscape archaeology and land history by Michael ('Mick') Aston, Batsford, reprinted 1995, paperback, £14.99.
This book contains an exceptionally useful overview of the processes and populations that have contributed to the shaping of the countryside.

A Slice through Time by M. G. L. Bailey, Batsford, 1995, paperback, £25.00.
Although the use of tree rings to map past environments is now fairly well known, it is little understood. This account describes the major uses and limitations of 'dendrochronology', and lists the types of environmental reconstructions that have been made possible by this means of dating.

The Archaeology of Disease by Charlotte Roberts and Keith Manchester, Alan Sutton Publishing, 2nd ed. 1995, hardback, £25.00.
A survey of the diseases and illnesses of early humans, which looks not only at their afflictions but also at the medicinal solutions offered in those times and, in cases of failure, the funerary practices. A truly intriguing study, accessible to both specialist and general reader.

Boleigh, Cornwall

The Southwest to AD 1000 by Malcolm Todd, Longman, 1987, paperback, £19.99.
The first full account of the Southwest of England from the first appearance of humans in the British Isles to the early Middle Ages. Todd focuses on the cultural continuity of the region, as well as the contacts with neighbouring cultures. A mine of fascinating local detail for anyone interested in this part of Britain.

Mother and Sun: The Cornish fogou by Ian McNeil Cooke, Menantol Studio, 1993, hardback £45.00 (a less expensive edition is planned).
A large volume containing numerous illustrations, this is *the* book on fogous. Cooke reviews previous work on all recorded examples and offers his own interpretation of their use.

Cornwall's Archaeological Heritage by N. Johnson and P. Rose, Cornwall Archaeological Unit, paperback, £3.50.
A visitor's booklet covering the region's most interesting archaeological features, including references to fogous.

Stanton Harcourt, Oxfordshire

Mammoths by Paul Bahn and Adrian Lister, Boxtree, 1995, hardback, £17.99.
Accurate, informative and accessible, this superbly illustrated account covers such aspects as the habitat and diet of the mammoth, skeletal excavation, mammoth-bone products, and cave paintings of these ancient beasts. For both archaeologists and general readers.

Life in the Ice Age by Anthony J. Stuart, Shire, 1988, paperback, £3.95.
A compact guide to these, the earliest days of human existence, giving information on many subjects, including climate and wildlife.

Timewalkers by Clive Gamble, Penguin, 1995, paperback, £8.99.
Newly available in paperback, this important work reviews our understanding of the spread of humans across the globe, and the development of the human behaviour that instigated that spread.

Prehistoric Life by William Lindsay, Dorling Kindersley, 1994, hardback, £8.99.
A lavishly illustrated guide to the origins of life on earth, from single-celled bacteria to dinosaurs and humans. Readable and informative, this is aimed at younger readers – and the young at heart.

Templecombe, Somerset

The Knight in Medieval England by Peter Coss, Alan Sutton Publishing, 1995, paperback, £9.99.
New in paperback, this book brings together current knowledge on the role of the knight in medieval society, from his origins and evolution in Saxon/Norman times to his place in literature and the social order.

The Book of the Medieval Knight by Stephen Turnbull, Arms & Armour, 1985, paperback, £14.99.
As much an introductory history of the 14th and 15th centuries as an account of English knighthood, this illustrated account examines the changing nature of warfare and chivalry in Britain and France.

Monasteries by Michael ('Mick') Aston, Batsford, 1993, paperback, £14.99.
An introduction examining the place of monasteries in the British landscape and their influence upon it. Mick Aston explains how monasticism arrived and developed in Britain, why abbeys and priories were built where they were, and what involvement they had with surrounding areas.

The Military Orders by Alan Forey, Macmillan, 1992, hardback, £13.50.
Focusing on the emergence and establishment of military orders from the 12th century onwards, this account examines the way in which they were able to obtain considerable funds and reserves of manpower, and the relationship between their lay and religious objectives.

Teignmouth, Devon

Burton's Bounty (£3.00) and **The Bronze Guns of Teignmouth, Ancient Maritime Town** (£5.50)
Two helpful guides, closely related to topics dealt with by TIME TEAM, published by Teignmouth Museum and Historical Society and available from: V. Wilson, Teignmouth Museum, 29 French Street, Teignmouth TQ14 8ST.

Archaeology Underwater, edited by M. Dean, B. Ferrari, I. Oxley, M. Redknap and K. Watson, Nautical Archaeological Society, reprinted 1995, paperback, £25.00.
Although a little technical, this detailed and well-illustrated reference book spells out the rules, techniques and challenges involved in finding and recording submerged archaeological material.

Navan, County Armagh

Pagan Celtic Ireland by Barry Raftery, Thames & Hudson, 1994, hardback, £24.00.
Using the latest archaeological information, this book presents an up-to-date account of Ireland in the millennium before the coming of Christianity, and discusses the social, artistic and ritual involvements of the Celtic peoples.

Exploring the World of the Celts by Simon James, Thames & Hudson, 1993, hardback, £16.95.
A brilliantly illustrated introduction to the world of the Celts, this looks at all aspects of their way of life and history, including their wars, religion and superb craftmanship, as well as their relations with the Romans and other peoples.

The Celtic Heroic Age by John T. Koch and John Carey, Celtic Studies, 2nd ed. 1995, paperback, £17.50.
Aimed at those with little knowledge of Celtic literature, this book contains translated material on and by the Celts from a number of sources, and provides a fascinating insight into their legends and heroes.

The Táin, translated by Thomas Kinsella, Oxford University Press, 1970, paperback, £8.99.
Written in about the 8th century, this is Ireland's greatest epic. Kinsella has used the earliest sources for his translation, and the result is an enjoyable read.

Lavenham, Suffolk

The Archaeology of Roman Suffolk by I. E. Moore, J. Plouviez and S. West, Suffolk County Council, 1988, £6.00.
A useful little book on the finds and sites of Suffolk, by the county's own archaeologists – those who know most about the subject.

The Finds of Roman Britain by Guy de la Bédoyère, Batsford, 1989, paperback, £14.99.
Written in non-specialist English, this is a well-illustrated guide to the various Roman finds from sites across the country, placing them within their social context.

Roman Vessel Glass by H. E. M. Cool and Jennifer Price, Colchester Archaeological Report 8, 1995, hardback, £24.00.
This technical report provides a broad overview of the glass in use in Roman Britain, as well as a detailed catalogue of dated finds.

The Hoxne Treasure by Roger Bland and Catherine Johns, British Museum Press, 1993, paperback, £4.95.
An introduction to and pictures of one of the richest late Roman hoards found some years ago in Suffolk.

CHANNEL FOUR TELEVISION

Published in 1996 by Channel 4 Television, 124 Horseferry Road, London SW1P 2TX
Produced by Broadcasting Support Services to accompany TIME TEAM
(a Video Text Communications production for Channel 4, in association with Diverse Production),
first shown on Channel 4 in January–February 1996.

TIME TEAM gratefully acknowledges the provision of Ordnance Survey digital maps for use on
TIME TEAM programmes.

Channel 4 Television and the TIME TEAM would like to thank
Chris Lynn, Phil Harding and Nick Johnson for their help in the creation of this booklet.

Editor: Paula Snyder
Editorial consultant: Nancy Duin
Site updates: Victoria Batten
Design: BIG-i, London
Illustrations: Nick Pearson
Printer: Haynes Cannon
Distributed by Broadcasting Support Services

Broadcasting Support Services provides follow-up services for viewers
and listeners and runs long-term helplines.

BSS

For further copies, please send a cheque or postal order for £3.75
(made payable to Channel 4 Television) to:

TIME TEAM 96

PO Box 4000, London W5 2GH or Cardiff CF5 2XT